For Nick,
Thanks for all your help
on the book!
your friend
Jan

LEGACY
of a
MONARCH

~ an American Journey ~

Jan Sumner

JD
JADAN PUBLISHING
Denver, Colorado

Legacy of a Monarch: an American Journey
By Jan Sumner

Published by:
JaDan Publishing
P.O. Box 22198
Denver, CO 80222

Cover & Interior design/layout NZ Graphics, www.nzgraphics.com

Photo on the front cover came from the family of Fred Swinton, who was one of the boys seated.

Library of Congress Control Number: 2005902271

ISBN: 0-9703197-5-4

DEDICATION

It's always a little tricky dedicating a book. Mothers, fathers, wives, best friends, contributors, etc. The list can get long and tangled. Here, for instance, I could pick any number of family members who contributed to my sanity and offered never-ending support through this project. And, certainly there were individuals in Byron's life who were deserving of such a tribute.

The more I thought about it, however, the more obvious the choice became. The picture on the front cover says it all. Byron is farthest left in the second row. You would only know that because I just told you. Who then, are the rest of the men and boys in the picture? We don't know. Oh, we could find out, probably, with extensive research, but that's the point.

The men pictured represent the hundreds of Negro League players who played anywhere from one game to thousands of games...and no one knows who they were. That's who this book is dedicated to. The nameless faces and jerseys that criss-crossed this country playing the game they loved. Putting up with hardship and racism we can only imagine.

Sadly, most have passed on, left only to family memories and archival pictures and articles. Still unknown, but staring hauntingly out at us from faded worn out paper. These are the men of Negro League baseball...the ghosts of an era gone by.

I was honored to write this book and I salute them one and all!

Jan Sumner

FOREWORD

This book will introduce you to an exceptional man who lived during a fascinating time. Byron Johnson is the grandson of a slave who overcame financial and social obstacles on his way to a college degree and a life devoted to education and to making the world a better place.

Byron Johnson grew up in Little Rock, in a segregated society, getting a college degree at a time when many institutions of higher education were closed to minorities. He became a biology teacher and was so dedicated to helping young people that he turned down the first offer he received to play professional baseball.

Byron became a great athlete in the Negro Leagues, known throughout the baseball world for his peerless defensive skills. He played for the Kansas City Monarchs, alongside legends like Satchel Paige and Buck O'Neil.

Then, while still in good enough shape to play many more years, Byron left his beloved baseball career to return to teaching. He also served in World War II, fighting to protect the freedoms that his country did not fully grant him.

Byron Johnson spent his life striving for greatness, both athletically and intellectually, and striving to instill it in others. He was a pioneer, paving the way for African Americans to enjoy equal rights and equal opportunities. Without Negro Leaguers like Byron demonstrating the extent of their skills, Major League Baseball would have taken much longer to integrate. Without educators like Byron, our nation's young people would not have had desperately needed role models to mold their characters and challenge their intellects. I am grateful for his inspiring life.

President Bill Clinton
February 2005

INTRODUCTION

Byron Johnson is a gentle man with an open hand and easy smile. Extremely approachable, he has a gracious manner and dignified demeanor.

He is not angry; he is not bitter.

What is obvious is that he is giving. And what he did was endure. Through their intensity on the playing field, and their ability to endure, the men of the Negro Leagues steadily chipped away at the wall of baseball segregation. In so doing, they paved the way for people like myself. As a major league baseball player from the generation of the 1970s, and as a major league manager of the 21st century, the Negro Leagues' history and ballplayers have inspired me throughout my career. I am filled with pride at their enduring, even while recognition of the significance of their efforts has been a "long time coming." Their contribution to the modern game has been too often overlooked and undervalued. Their determination, however, lives on through myself and all other ballplayers of color who have benefited from the continued success of professional baseball.

In the world of strict racial segregation in which he was born, begun in Jim Crow Arkansas, the struggle and primary goal for "Mex" Johnson and his contemporaries was simply to reach the playing field, and to show that their physical abilities matched those of their white counterparts. By now it's infamously well documented that disputing, or even worse, daring to attempt to prove wrong, the commonly held belief that black ballplayers were incapable of competing for any position on the field brought derision, scorn and often violence. The struggle that began more than 130 years ago to be recognized on the basis of merit and on a "level playing field" continues well into the 21st century. Even as racial barriers to athletic participation have come tumbling down in the past 50 years, while encouraged by the accomplishments, we must remain vigilant about the challenges that lie ahead. As one of a handful of African-American managers, I assume this responsibility with sincere humility, knowing what sacrifices others, especially Negro Leaguers, made to give me the opportunity to play, let alone manage in the major leagues.

The unfolding of "Mex" Johnson's life is truly a testament to the human spirit when faced with adverse circumstances and rigid barriers. As a grandson of a slave, Johnson embodied the strides that African-Americans had made during the span of two generations. A husband, scholar, citizen, teacher, soldier, father and two-sport athlete, Johnson forced his peers to think of him in multiple ways. His willingness to serve stands out as the most impressive theme running throughout his remarkable life. As a World War II veteran, joining the fight for freedom in a foreign nation (and liberties he did not enjoy in his own home state) speaks to his character and enduring hope for a better America. And, as a person who believed to his core in "giving back," Byron rarely shunned an opportunity to transfer his knowledge to the persons most in need of a role model: our youth. He firmly understood that the permanent legacy of the African-American athlete would lie in our ability to teach life lessons to these young men and women for whom our stature commands so much of their attention.

As an individual in the public eye and one of the caretakers of a legacy laid down by trailblazers of Mex Johnson's era, I continue to absorb their lessons with the awareness of the need to keep this history alive for younger generations. And, as a coach and manager, the knowledge of this history keeps me equally committed to impressing younger players of the power our prestige can exert as a positive influence. I, too, believe in giving back.

It's important to me that we honor Byron Johnson and the men like him by listening to his story. We owe these men a debt of gratitude and we all need to pay attention. I'm sure Byron would agree, so we can "pass it on."

Don Baylor
October 2004

1

In 1911, ragtime composer Scott Joplin composed *Treemonisha*, an opera extolling the virtues of education for black Americans. It was read in Harlem in 1916, without the use of an orchestra or scenery. With the decline of ragtime and Joplin's health, it would not be premiered until sixty-one years later in January of 1972 in Atlanta, Georgia.

Ty Cobb won the first MVP award in the American League, Honus Wagner won the National League batting crown by one point, and Cy Young beat Pittsburgh 1-0 for his 511th and last career win. The son of a minister, Andrew Foster, went into partnership with John Schorling, the son-in-law of Charles Comiskey, and arrange for a black baseball team to play in old Chicago White Sox Park. Andrew "Rube" Foster would rename them the Chicago American Giants and a dynasty was born. It was a team that would become a dominant force in Negro League baseball for years, and one Byron "Mex" Johnson would play against twenty-seven years later.

The house was on the edge of town, next to a field with ditches and pine trees...lots of pine trees. It was built by his father, Joseph, so that Byron might be born at home. One of nine children, he was the youngest and the only child in the family that would make his earthly appearance at 4423 W. 16th Street in Little Rock, Arkansas.

"I came along and rounded out the mighty Johnson family," Byron said proudly. "We were a happy family because we all loved each other. Even though my sisters were married and gone, they would still come back to see us. I cherished those days we were all together." Whether it was the fact he was born there, grew up there or maybe it was those old pine trees, but this was and would always be home to Byron.

His father was a painter, born in 1869 outside Montgomery, Alabama. Little is known about that side of the family, other than his grandparents were Coffee Louis and Sara Johnson and they lived out most of their lives in Alabama. But throughout his life his father would play a major role in Byron's existence. "Who was really the best to me was my dad. He was my hero, especially after my mother died." His mother, Elizabeth

Golden, was born in Batesville, Arkansas as the daughter of a slave. Her mother, Betty Golden, kept house and tended to the children of rich white families. Her father was a white doctor in Batesville who, although never admitting to his paternity, was nonetheless active in their lives.

The neighborhood Byron grew up in was predominantly black, with a sprinkling of white families. For the most part everyone got along, as long as they knew their place. Little Rock was definitely a southern segregated city. Byron would learn over the years what everybody's place was. One of these white families lived directly behind the Johnsons'.

Horatius was the first-born son in the Johnson family, but they called him "Bud". Bud, raised chickens, as many did back then. "People back then, in that part of Little Rock, had horses, a few cows, some hogs, and everyone had chickens," Byron recalled. Bud had just gotten home from World War I and set about tending to his chickens. "I was glad to see him. I had just broken my arm trying to jump on the swing in the front yard."

Somehow one of Bud's chickens got into the yard of the white lady who lived behind them. She apparently didn't have, didn't like, and wanted nothing to do with chickens, so she went after it. She hit it in the head with a dirt clod, but didn't kill it. While it was squawking and flopping around on the ground hurt, Bud couldn't contain himself. He leapt over the fence, grabbed the chicken, and regrettably (for Bud) slapped the white woman. Mr. Finn, an elderly white man in the neighborhood, caught wind of the incident and vowed that Bud would pay for his indiscretion. Joseph Johnson put Bud on a train out of town that same night. Byron would not see Bud again until he was a grown man playing baseball for the Kansas City Monarchs thirty years later.

His father, whom Byron affectionately called "Papa", was a house painter by trade. His mother was a teacher. "Mama was a schoolteacher, and she taught in a small school house just outside of Little Rock. The school house was no bigger than the small houses around it. She drove a horse and buggy to get there, and sometimes she'd take me with her. I remember that old horse was named Charlie. She taught first through twelfth grade...all in that little house."

Byron had five brothers, all of whom painted at one time or another, as per Papa's penchant. Horatius (Bud) was the oldest, followed by Louis, then Clayborn, then Mark and Earl. "Louis was a real like-able fellow," Byron recalled. "He was real easy to be around. I remember right after he died, I was standing on 18th and Vine in Kansas City, when an old man came up to me looking like he'd seen a ghost. He looked at me and said, 'Lord, I heard Mr. Johnson had passed, but when I looked out my window and saw you I'd have sworn I was looking right at him.' He had mistaken me for Louis and came down to see."

Clayborn was next in line and became somewhat the historian of the family. He was a loner, studious and liked to keep to himself. Although quiet and reserved, he was always there with a helping hand. "When they weren't going to let me graduate from Wiley because I still owed some money, Clayborn sent what I needed. We called him Doc."

Next was brother Mark. His full name was Mark Theodore Roosevelt Johnson; they called him "Tootie". He, too, was quiet, didn't say much, but didn't put up with much either. "I heard he was in the barber shop one day, when some fellow started talking out of place to a lady who was in there. The way I heard it, whatever he was saying wasn't right, but no one would do anything about it. Next thing anybody knew Mark had gotten up out of his chair, walked over to the man and flattened him, then went back to his chair, sat down and never said a word. Yeah, that was Mark. We didn't look alike when we were young, but when we got in our sixties, we started looking a lot like Papa."

Then came Earl; they called him "Possum". He and Byron looked so much alike people constantly got them confused. They would share some good and some sad times together.

His three sisters were Sadie, the oldest, whom he doesn't remember a lot about because she was married and gone when Byron was born. "The thing I most remember about Sadie, was the wide gray streak in her hair. It ran from her forehead down the full length of her hair. She also made me an uncle when I was still a little baby. Her oldest son Alvin and I are about three months apart. The only other memory I have is of her funeral. I was the only one in the family that could get there..."

Then there was Helen, whom Byron would live with briefly after his mother died. Finally there was Mabel. "I don't remember much about my sisters because they were all older and grown and gone while I was growing up."

Byron would be the last surviving member of the Johnson siblings, and sadly the only one able to attend the funeral of each of his brothers and sisters.

In 1912, W.C. Handy wrote the first blues song ever published, *"The Memphis Blues."* The Titanic sank on its maiden voyage across the Atlantic, and Byron Johnson would, at the age of one, find his life in peril on a train ride from Arkansas to Illinois.

2

The year was 1838, and the Principal People, as they called themselves, were being dragged from their homes, beaten and murdered, and about to start on one of the most arduous journeys in American history. They were the Cherokee Indians, and it was the beginning of the end of their nation, as they had known it...The Trail of Tears.

This journey would take them from Red Clay and Ross's Landing, in Georgia and Tennessee, to Ft. Gibson in the Indian Territory (Oklahoma). Slaves from Alabama and Georgia would join this march, suffering the same indignities and brutality as the Cherokee. One of these slave families were the Johnsons. For reasons unknown they stopped in Arkansas and would eventually settle in Little Rock.

"We don't know if someone got sick, or they found

some work there, but they did stop there. My great, grandfather, Coffee Louis Johnson, actually bought some land in Alabama in 1866 during the Reconstruction," remembered Jacquelyn Benton, Byron's daughter.

Sadly, as was so often the case, any history or records of both Indian and slave families was lost or more than likely never recorded. This was certainly true of Byron's family. There was gossip within the family that part of their lineage had in fact originated from a Southern general during the Civil War. When told of this Byron said, "Hold it right there! I don't want to hear any of this." Bowing to his wishes, it was dropped, but there is a natural curiosity that remains. Due to the contingencies of the time, nothing could ever be proved.

By the early 1880s the Johnson family had put down roots in Arkansas. In New York, with a bustling population of 250,000, a game was being played called Base Ball. Players would meet at Madison Square, where Fifth Avenue and Broadway meet at 23rd street, play this new game and argue about what rules to use. The game had recast itself into many versions, but what Union soldiers took with them into the Civil War was the New York version. After four long years of war, armies of the North and South scattered across the country taking Base Ball with them. It was a game Byron would learn to love and play.

"To tell you the truth it seems like I've played baseball all my life in one way or another," Byron said warmly. "In my day every vacant lot would turn into a baseball field, so I started playing sandlot ball early. One of my first baseballs was a Coca-Cola top, the same top they put on bottles today. An old broom handle was usually my bat. When we'd hit that cap, it would bend the edges, and man, that top would take off. My next ball was made of balled up white paper. We'd take kite cord or twine and wind it around tight to make a ball. We had lots of fun."

Baseball would become more important as Byron grew older, but while he was young, education and church were the governing factors in his life. His mother was emphatic about both. School was a must, and baseball should not, could not, and would not be played on Sundays.

Elizabeth Johnson was a woman of strong will and conviction. Being the daughter of a slave, she had plenty of grit and determination. "They said she was taking a train to Cairo, Illinois, to see my sister, Sadie," Byron recalled. "She took me with her, I was about one year old. The train got robbed and Mama hid me under her petticoats so the robbers wouldn't see me. Isn't that something?"

Byron would also remember her standing behind the stove cooking, washing clothes in a big tub in the back yard, and working in the garden. But what he would remember most was her death. "She died on May 8, 1921, I was nine years old. If you look on the calendar you'll see that it was Mother's Day. I had made a little greeting card at school, and I remember on that Friday the teacher said, ' Don't let your mother see your card until Mother's Day.' I held on to my card like the teacher said, but unfortunately for me my mother died around four in the morning...she never got to see my little card. Now, that hurt me, and I would have to say, affects me still. She never got to see my Mother's Day card...."

The loss of his mother at such an early age would have a profound effect on Byron's life. Part of the reason he always stayed on the straight and narrow path was because, even though she was dead, he knew in his heart he'd disappoint her if he strayed from her teachings.

"After my mother died, I remember all the people coming over cooking, cleaning the house, trying to help Papa. Somebody hung a black wreath on the front door...I didn't like looking at it. I watched when the undertakers from Dubisson's came to get her. After they brought her back I would go in the living room and just look at her. In those days the body stayed in the house until it was time for the funeral.

"I don't remember the funeral, but I know I was there. It was at Wesley Chapel in Little Rock. I remember going by Philander Smith College (where Christine, his future wife, would go to college) on the long journey to the church. I also remember seeing my friend Kermit, standing out in the street as we went by. He just stared at me. Funny, I remember those things, but can't remember the funeral itself. I just know that after my mother was gone, those were some sad, sad days in my life."

The Black poet Langston Hughes had his first poem, *"The Negro Speaks of Rivers,"* published in 1921. The Negro National League, founded by Rube Foster, was scheduled to start play, while just nine years earlier; Ty Cobb had gone into the stands and savagely beat a heckler, Claude Lueker, for calling him a "half nigger." Cobb's teammates on the Detroit Tigers refused to play after his suspension, even though they had no use for him, other than as a ballplayer, because they said, "That it was too big an insult for any white man to bear."

A few years later Byron would get to hear Langston Hughes speak at his high school in Little Rock, and by his twenty-sixth birthday he would be playing in the Negro National League. There was also a tall, lanky pitcher beginning to make a name for himself in black baseball. Satchel Paige would not only go on to become, maybe the greatest pitcher in history, but one of Byron's closest friends.

3

"I think it was the women in the community, maybe from the church, who decided that Earl and I should leave," Byron said. "I know Papa wasn't crazy about separating the family, but Earl and I were the youngest, and I guess the women felt it would be best that we go live with our sisters after my mothers death. So Earl went to Mabel in Helena, Arkansas, and I went to Helen in Kansas City, Missouri. I remember that Helen had a big, pretty house, and when you went out her front door, the porch led right down to the sidewalk where all the cars were shooting by...I didn't like that."

After his mother's death, Byron felt displaced, lonely. He missed his dad, Earl, his friends at Stephens Elementary School, and the activities at White Memorial Methodist Church in Little Rock. He also missed his home; "I loved those woods, and I guess I knew just about every rock and tree out there."

A few weeks went by, and although he was only nine years old, he'd had enough. It wasn't that Helen wasn't kind and caring; it was just too painful being away from home. "I wrote Papa a letter, and I told him if he didn't come to get me I was coming home by myself. Later he told me, 'Johnbrownit, I thought you might be fool enough to try it!' So he came by train to get me. I was the happiest kid in the world to be going home with my dad. The first thing I did was write Earl a letter telling him what I'd done. It wasn't long before Papa was getting another letter and taking another train trip. Earl met me grinning, and that's how we got back together again."

The next two years would be secure for Byron, as Papa did everything in his power to make up for the loss of Byron's mother. He immersed himself in school, church and started playing lots of baseball with his brothers, and/or anyone else he could find to play with. Every field and vacant lot became a big league baseball diamond. Even at this early age, he was beginning to hone his skills as a smooth-fielding shortstop.

Baseball had come out of the 1919 Black Sox scandal riding the shoulders of one George Herman "Babe" Ruth. In 1921, he hit an astounding 59 home runs. Meanwhile, the Kansas City, Monarchs would go 50-31 and play, in essence, what was the first Negro

League World Series against Rube Foster's Chicago American Giants. Negro League ball also had its first budding star, a big, strong, malicious man named Oscar Charleston. He would dominate Negro ball for many years, and he was compared to Babe Ruth for his thunderous home runs. It was also one of the most profound years in the history of the game, as the Supreme Court ruled baseball was a sport and not a business, therefore not subject to anti-trust laws. In 1923, President Warren Harding died of a heart attack, and African American choreographer Elida Webb set off an international dance craze when she introduced the Charleston in a New York City music and dance show, *"Runnin' Wild."*

A little over a year and a half after Byron's mother died, his dad married Estella Goodwin. She was much younger than his dad, which immediately brought friction to the family.

"Papa married Estella Goodwin about two years after Mama died and my sisters stopped coming to see us. They were mad because of the marriage, and now I can understand why they would have been. Papa was almost thirty years older than Miss Stella, which didn't make her a whole lot younger than my sister Sadie, or older than me. Miss Stella must have had some problems with my brothers too, because I can remember Papa telling them, 'This is my home, and now it's Stell's home. You don't have to love her, but if you stay here, you're going to respect her.' They stayed, but I know Miss Stella always felt that the family didn't want her. After Miss Stella came, her cousin Bertie lived with us for a while too. I remember Bertie because of my cedar tree. I found a cedar tree in the woods one day and dug it up. When I brought it home, I planted it right in the front of the house, right where the coalhouse used to be. I was planning to grow birds in that tree, so I put some chicken wire around it. The tree would be the roost for the birds. I remember when Bertie saw that little tree she said, 'When that tree gets high enough for its shadow to cover your grave, you gon' die!' I never did forget that, and I know some time later I saw that tree throwing out a shadow. Boy, I wondered if I should cut that sucker down...but I didn't. The last time I was in Little Rock that cedar tree was still standing, and it had grown tall enough for its shadow to cover EVERYBODY'S grave."

With discord at home and the ever-impending threat of death from the budding cedar tree, Byron sank his spikes into baseball. He loved the game, and the people who watched him play loved the way he played the game. There was only one problem, Sunday!

"The first team I played on was called The Bee's. We'd have about fourteen or fifteen on the team. An old baseball player put the team together, and he was our first manager. A step up was playing on the men's team, and I got to do that after I met Duncan Ingram. Duncan was a friend of my brother Earl and was always at our house. He was a carpenter and walked with a limp, but boy, could that man play baseball. I was about thirteen when I met him. He was about five years older than me, but he spent a lot of time with me and taught me what he knew about baseball. He was the shortstop for a team called Highline Sports. I wanted to play for them so bad I didn't know what to do.

"One day something happened and Duncan could not play, so he talked the manager into letting me fill in for him. I guess I did all right, because afterward I remember somebody telling Duncan, 'Man, you better watch out, Mex gon' take your job.'"

"In Little Rock, everybody called me "Mex". I used to hitch my little wagon to my goat, Billy Boy, and head out to the baseball field. I'd always be wearing a black hat that had a wide brim with red tassels all around it. My dad bought that hat for me, and I guess it kind of looked like a sombrero. People started calling me Mex, and the name stuck. Anyway, Highline Sports wanted me to play for them after I filled in for Duncan, but my people wouldn't let me, because the team played on Sunday."

Sunday was for church, religious reflection...not

baseball. Byron would eventually solve this problem through sly tactics and prayer.

It was 1924, and Louis Armstrong made his first recording, *"Everybody Loves My Baby."* J. Edgar Hoover became the newly appointed head of the Bureau of Investigation, which in 1935 became the FBI. He would remain in power for the next 48 years, during which time he'd conduct investigations and surveillance on people like, Eleanor Roosevelt, Supreme Court Justice William O. Douglas and Martin Luther King Jr., all based on his analysis of what represented a threat to America. In Russia, Lenin died and the general secretary of the Communist Party, Joseph Stalin, came to power.

This was also the year J.L. Wilkinson surpassed Rube Foster in the ever-changing landscape of black baseball. His Kansas City Monarchs were asserting themselves as the epitome of the Negro Leagues. Wilkinson had become exceedingly proficient at picking talent. Some of his more significant finds were second baseman Newt Allen, third baseman Newt Joseph, and an amazing young pitcher, "Bullet" Joe Rogan.

Little did a teenage shortstop in Little Rock, Arkansas know that several years later he would share some exciting, dramatic, and frightening moments with these very same men.

4

"My first job was delivering papers, then I moved up to cutting grass, then I delivered milk. By the time I got to high school I started delivering groceries. My dad had always been a hard worker, and I only remember him being self-employed. Most of his friends were self-employed too, brick layers, carpenters, trades like that. Through all those jobs though, he always found a way to stick a paintbrush in my hand. It seemed like I was always helping him paint a house. That was okay though, I think it made me a good worker...not afraid to work."

Byron had only played baseball by the time he hit high school. Church, school, job, family and baseball (except Sundays) had been the extent of his life to that point. High school would be a new awakening, a broader horizon...football, girls, and baseball on SUNDAYS!

"When I got to high school, I started playing football. I went to Dunbar High School, named after the poet, Paul Laurence Dunbar. I was in the class of 1931. There were only three boys and eighteen girls in the class...so you know we had a ball. Two of us boys were on the football team, and I was the quarterback. We never had new, or much, equipment to play with, but during my senior year, the white high school gave us their old uniforms...but no helmets. Since we didn't have enough helmets, Robert Waugh and I played in our baseball caps.

"We had an excellent coach by the name of John Arthur Hibler. He taught us football from a scientific standpoint. I always compare Hibler to Big Long, my football coach at Wiley College. Big Long believed in getting over on your opponent by brute strength, so naturally he liked big men. Where, Hibler taught us to out think our opponents, and use psychology on them. Hibler also treated his quarterback like a king, so he never kicked me. You know in the those days some coaches would beat up on their men. Big Long would kick All-Americans! Now that I think about it, maybe that had something to do with my wanting to be a quarterback. I know I didn't want nobody beating on me, but, I was always Hibler's main man.

"You know, it's odd, but after all these years I can still remember some of the plays I'd call. Like if I called 5-2-3-4-1-4, the first number was the man carrying the ball, the third was the hole, and the last was the number the ball would be snapped on. I guess I had a unique cadence in the way I called the play, because years after my high school days, I was in Fort Smith at a party out in the yard when a fellow came by in a car, stopped in the middle of the street, got out and yelled something like, 'Threee-two-four-five-twoooo!' I turned around and looked, he said, 'It's me Mex.' Now I didn't know who 'me' was, but it turned out to be one of the players for Fort Smith we used to play against, and he remembered how I called those signals back in high school.

"Now, my people were never crazy about me playing football, so, I told Papa one day, 'I know y'all don't want me to play football, so if I can just play baseball on Sundays, I'll give up football.' Well, I must've been using Coach Hibler's psychology on him, because I ended up doing both. That's how I got to play baseball with Highline Sports...on Sundays."

His first year in high school, 1929, the stock market crashed, setting off the Great Depression. It would take over a decade for the economy, and the country, to recover. By the time it was over, Byron would be winding down his career with the Satchel Paige All-Stars. Just two years earlier Babe Ruth had hit an astonishing sixty home runs. One year prior to that,

Ty Cobb, the man who went into the stands and beat a man senseless, for being called a "half nigger," retired. By 1930, Ruth would sign a contract for an even more astounding $80,000. The average salary for a major league player in 1930 was $7,000. On December 9, 1930, Rube Foster, the true founder of the Negro Leagues, died of a heart attack at the age of fifty-one. By Byron's junior year there were four million unemployed people in the United States. Fortunately, his dad was not one of them. "It really didn't affect us much. We always had something to eat, and a good place to sleep."

The other two boys in Byron's graduating class were Robert Waugh and Oscar "Horace" Berry. They went on to become All-American football players at Langston College. Byron had a chance to go with them, but opted to stay home. "I guess I was too much of a 'Homeboy.' I didn't want to leave Little Rock."

As a teenager growing up in a southern segregated city, Byron's activities consisted of his sports, church activities and socials at school. They also went to lots of movies, lots of cowboy movies, on Saturday evenings. The staggering price of admission was five and ten cents, depending on the movie and time of day. "We always traveled as a group, 'cause, if you got caught alone…well, you'd be in serious trouble." Trouble was in the form of white packs of teenagers or the police.

"We had to sit upstairs at the movies, no doubt about it." Those were the rules in the South and even the Midwest. Should a black person venture downstairs, either accidentally or with intention, he or she was escorted unceremoniously out of the theater. But beyond all this there was an even more fetching reason to stay home...Christine Torrence. Byron and Christine had gone all through school together, attended the same church and social affairs. "I always made sure I walked with Christine's group to and from church and school." He was smitten with her from the beginning. Years later she would tell noted Negro League historian, Jay Sanford, "I really didn't care about Byron...until he started playing quarterback on the football team in high school."

Byron was playing baseball now on Sundays, but Christine could not come. Apparently the Hibler psychology hadn't worked on her parents, so he would meet her at church Sunday nights, and then walk her home. They all lived within a few blocks of each other on the west side of Little Rock. The theater and drug store were about eight miles away. Those were always pack trips, as in numbers. On the other hand if the white kids came below 16th street, they could be in some severe trouble. And yet, with this constant cloak of bigotry hanging over them, there was one genial white family that lived close to Byron, "I grew up playing with the three white boys, stayed in their home, slept and ate with them, but we had to go to separate schools. There was a swimming pool for the white kids, but we had to swim in the ditches and canals."

Dunbar had added a junior college program to their curriculum so upon graduation from high school, Byron enrolled at Dunbar Jr. College. By now he was seriously into baseball, playing for the Little Rock All-Stars, also known as the Black Travelers. This was Arkansas's first and only all black pro team playing in the Negro Southern League.

"I didn't play baseball in Jr. high, high school or college, just in the summers, but it was my favorite sport. I can't remember not having a baseball in my hand. Every vacant lot was converted into a baseball diamond back then, but the main parks with bleachers were Kavanaugh Field, which is where Earl Quigley Stadium now sits, Crump's Field, which was at 33rd and State streets in south Little Rock, and Travelers Field, which became Ray Winder Field.

"Crump's Field was mainly for black players. The first time I ever played against big leaguers was in that park. It was 1932, and I was playing for the Little Rock Stars. The Pittsburgh Crawfords, along with several stars from other teams, were on their way to Hot Springs, Arkansas to use the hot baths. They stopped in Little Rock to play an exhibition game against us.

"This was the best team and some of the best ballplayers in Negro ball. They had Oscar Charleston, Cool Papa Bell, Ted "Double Duty" Radcliffe catching, and Josh Gibson. As I remember, they beat us," Byron said laughing.

That same year at Wrigley Field, in Chicago, Babe Ruth "called his shot" in the World Series against the Chicago Cubs. At 37, this would be his last great year. In Macon County, Alabama the U.S. Public Health Service began a forty-year syphilis experiment using 300 black men as subjects, without their knowledge. It was called the Tuskegee Syphilis Study, to examine the morbidity and mortality among untreated victims by withholding known drug therapies. Joseph Stalin had come to full power in the USSR, by imprisoning 12 million and executing 7 million others. In Germany, Adolph Hitler's Nazi Party emerged as a political force.

By 1933, the Little Rock Stars had folded, and Byron would play and manage a team called the Dubisson Tigers in Little Rock. He also graduated from Dunbar Jr. College and was about to step away from home and everything he loved and head to a little dusty spot on the map, Marshall, Texas, and football again, at Wiley College.

5

"Several days before I left for Wiley College, I was packing stuff up in my room. Miss Stella came in with a look of terror on her face. She'd been cleaning Mark's room, he was my 'peculiar' brother, liked to stay to himself, she had been pulling off his bed sheets when she heard something hit the floor. She looked down to see a .45 pistol lying on the floor. She told me, 'I'm never goin' back in that room again.'"

Byron's mother had been a teacher and was resolute on getting an education. So, too, was Stella. She encouraged him to go to, and finish college. It had been a test for her, a younger woman, trying to fill in for an adored, deceased mother. But she had a good heart and tried to do the right thing. "I remember the Brooks family came to live with us, because they had nowhere else to stay. I think they stayed with us about a year, there were a bunch of them, and they all had to stay in one room. Then another time she took in three boys for a while, and one of them went on to become a bank president or something. I know she had a tough time of it...but I always liked her."

In the summer of 1933, Byron was managing and playing shortstop for the Dubisson Tigers. (Dubisson sponsored the team and was also the funeral home that buried his mother, twelve years earlier). They traveled the South playing in Texarkana, Forest City, Pine Bluff, New Orleans, Memphis, and Shreveport. While playing in New Orleans, he was spotted by Coach Long from Wiley College. Impressed with Byron's great arm strength, and bogus bulk, he offered him a football scholarship. "I was just 5'8", 145 pounds, so when I played baseball I wore lots of pads...you know, so I'd look bigger."

Apparently, Fred "Pop" Long, also known as "Big", hadn't bothered to really check Byron's enhanced musculature out, because once he got to campus...well, let's just say Big Long was "Big" disappointed. "When he saw me he was real mad, he cursed everyone in sight. He told me, 'If I'd known you were this small, I'd never have given you a scholarship.'"

What Coach Long wasn't able to see under those simulated muscles, was Byron's heart and brains. He'd been well-schooled by coach Hibler at Dunbar High, remember the Hibler psychology, so now it was his turn to apply it to the coaching staff at Wiley.

"At first they put me on the third or fourth string, I didn't get to play much." But it wasn't long before Byron asserted himself in fundamentals and shrewdness and got the coaches' attention. "I remember the quarterbacks were having a skull session and Big Long asked, 'What determines what play you call?' I raised my hand, knew the answer, but he wouldn't call on me. After some dead silence, Little Long, Big Long's brother, said, 'Jewbaby [this would be a name that would stick with him through college. There are various versions of why, but no one seems to know for sure] what's your answer?' I said, 'When I go to the line of scrimmage, I look to see what holes the defense is lined up in, and look for some other things, not wanting the other quarterbacks to know what they were.' Little Long just smiled. They moved me up to first string."

Wiley was an all-black, Methodist school, known for excellent academics and a good football program. Most of their students graduated as teachers, but they also had pre-med and a law school. Byron wanted to go into medicine, but couldn't afford it. In fact he couldn't even afford paying for school beyond his scholarship.

"I didn't have any money and couldn't get any financial help from my family, so after practice I'd run to the mess hall, without cleaning up, and serve the same players I'd just practiced with. I couldn't eat or take a shower till they were all done. This usually meant some cold food and always some cold water in the shower. I did that for a year...till I was worn out."

This same year, 1933, Major League Baseball and Negro League Baseball held their very first All-Star Games, both at Comiskey Park in Chicago. The black ball version was called the East-West Game. Sierra Leone-born dancer Asadata Dafora choreographed and presented *Kykunkor, The Witch Woman*, using a mixed cast of Africans and African Americans in a New York premiere. White audiences and critics commented on seeing a new view of Africans as humans instead of barbarians. Shocked, Dafora said, "Barbarism? But there are lynchings in this country."

Several of Byron's teammates on the football team played baseball in the summers. "Packinghouse" Adams played for several black semi-pro teams in the South, eventually playing some backup third base for the Kansas City Monarchs in 1938, the same year Byron would make the All-Star team. Another teammate, Andrew "Pat" Patterson, had a lengthy and successful career in the Negro Leagues. He played for various teams from 1934 to 1949, and two years, 1936 and 1941, with the Monarchs. He graduated from Wiley, and following his baseball career went into education, eventually becoming the superintendent of schools in Houston, Texas. As a running back for Wiley, Henry "Streak" Milton quickly became one of Byron's favorites. "I called him Little Man, cause he was small and fast. I mean that boy could fly," Byron commented. Little Man would be the leadoff hitter for the Monarchs during their dominant years and make the All-Star team five consecutive years, 1936-40. Sadly 1940 was his last season as a regular player and soon there after he was out of baseball. He died of spinal meningitis shortly after retiring still in his early thirties.

Although an all-black college, Wiley would bring in white guest lecturers to enhance the students' education...so to speak. One such guest was a white missionary, a woman there to talk about the great things she'd done with regard to bringing people into the church. "About this time Joe Louis was coming into his own as a fighter," Byron recalled. "She told us we were making strides as a race, but we still had our limits and should not marry whites, because we just weren't equal, and it wouldn't work. Professor Tolson, one of our English teachers, stood up in the auditorium and said to her, 'Madam, if you say we are not equal to you, you're talking a little late, because evidently, your ancestors didn't believe that, because if they had, we wouldn't be here today.' It grew dead silent, and the poor lady had to walk out through all the students."

The professor Tolson Byron spoke of was in fact, Melvin B. Tolson who taught at Wiley from 1924 until 1947, when he took a leave to pursue work in a Master's degree from Columbia University. He would emerge as a well-known poet and short story teller with *A Gallery of Harlem Portraits* being his most profound work. He moved on to Langston University in 1947, in Langston, Oklahoma, where he also served three terms as Mayor. He died in 1966 in Dallas, Texas after undergoing surgery for cancer.

Even though this was Byron's first year at Wiley, he was a junior in class standing. He started off with a major in math and a minor in chemistry. When coach Long found out he was taking math he said, "That damn Jew Baby's a fool." That, coupled with the fact he wanted to get out quick and, of course, the slight detail that Ralph Edmonson (math teacher) was the toughest instructor he'd ever had, made him change his major. He switched to education. The Dean of the school called him in and told him if he switched to education he could graduate immediately. "I told her, 'Whatever I have to do – I'll do it!'"

By 1936, Byron was ready to graduate, or so he thought. The Dean of the School, Dr. Dogan, however, informed him he was $40 short for graduation. If he could just come up with it, he'd get to hold that well-earned diploma. Byron didn't have it, and wasn't sure where to get it. Hearing of Byron's predicament, his brother Clayborn (Doc) came up with the $40, and sent it to him so he could depart Wiley, sheepskin in hand. "I was so grateful, not only for the money, but so I could get away from Wiley. I'd worked so hard, it was a relief just to go back home."

And home he went, back to Little Rock, back to Dunbar High School, this time as a teacher and coach. He taught science and coached football. He still played for the Dubisson Tigers, and that same summer, playing in a game in Shreveport, Louisiana, a scout for the Kansas City Monarchs spotted this slick-fielding shortstop who went by the nickname "Mex."

One year before Byron graduated, Babe Ruth had been released by the Yankees, then signed a three-year contract with the Braves, and on May 25 hit three home runs against Pittsburgh. He then retired a few days later, having hit a grand total of 714 home runs. Satchel Paige was nearing his peak and Joe Louis was one year from winning the heavyweight crown. Mussolini's Italian Fascist troops marched into Ethiopia, while Emperor Haile Selassie called for his people to fight for the survival of the only independent black state in Africa. The rest of the world watched with ambivalence. And Adolf Hitler opened the 1936 Olympic Games in Berlin. He left the stadium humiliated after African American Jesse Owens won four gold medals.

Jesse and Byron would cross paths later at Negro League baseball games, as Jesse was hired by owners and promoters for sideshow entertainment. But in 1936, even as the world quaked with the anticipation of war, a war that would be based on hatred and lust for power over others, blacks and whites found a place to coexist, even to the point of helping one another.

During the Olympic Games Jesse had scratched on his first two attempts at the long-jump. If he faltered on his third and last try, he would be disqualified. Lutz Long, a blond German long jumper, came to Jesse's aid.

"Jesse, let me place my sweater a foot in front of the foul line and use it as your take off point," Long said. "You can easily qualify if you do that."

Jesse not only qualified, but beat Long in the final. As Nazi leaders looked on, Jesse Owens, the son of a black Alabama sharecropper, and Long, the embodiment of Hitler's Aryan man, walked off the field together, arm in arm.

They stayed in contact until World War II when Long was shipped off to North Africa. Before his death, Long sent Owens a last letter.

"My heart tells me that if I am to be honest with you, this is the last letter that I will ever write. If it is so, I ask you to go to Germany when this war is done. Someday find my son Karl and tell him about his father. Tell him, Jesse, what times were like when we were separated by war. Tell him how things can be between men on this earth."

Jesse went to Berlin after the war, found Long's son, and eventually paid for his college education. He was also Karl Long's best man at his wedding eighteen years later.

6

His name was Roosevelt. A black man, mildly retarded, who did menial odd jobs around town. Nice, harmless, always willing to help. She was a huckster, peddling her wares from a horse drawn cart. Most days she'd make her rounds, selling a sundry of items to anyone and everyone who'd listen. This day was no different than any other, her wooden cart clomping down the street. Suddenly, the horse began to buck and rear, panicked. People began to turn, staring in horror. As the horse became more enraged, and bystanders continued to be bystanders, this quiet, unassuming black man ran across the street to help. His slow, but focused thoughts were about one thing only: help the woman in distress.

This was the late 1920s, Little Rock, Arkansas. Black men and white women did not mix...under any circumstances, even shared terror. As the horse continued to lurch, she began to scream. Roosevelt was doing his best to gain control of the horse, but with little success. The cart began to rock as the Good Samaritan attempted to come to the aid of the floundering woman.

"It was horrifying. It made the front page of the newspaper. I'll never forget it, till the day I die," Byron said in disbelief. "I knew him, he lived just down the street from us. He was just trying to..." Byron turned, looked out the bedroom window his eyes filling.

As was always the case back then, several white men, who were nowhere to be found earlier, came running to the aid of this white woman...being attacked by this crazed black man. Roosevelt ran; he was running for his life. Through the houses, down alleys, and eventually into the woods on the edge of town. "It was late fall, so all the trees were bare. He climbed one, but he couldn't hide," Byron remembered. "They shot him out of the tree, like some kind of animal."

They dragged him through town, dead, ropes around his legs. Dragged him into the black section of town, to his church. Leaving him in the street, they broke into the church, smashed the pews to use as firewood, then set the building on fire. As a final show of outrage, they threw Roosevelt on top of the blazing house of worship.

"They kept records of the lynchings," Byron's

daughter Jackie said, "But I guess since this wasn't officially a lynching, there was no record of it. I know I never found a record of it."

In the mid-1930s, there were more college graduates in the Negro Leagues, than in major league baseball. The country was coming out of its worst drought in history and the first night game in the majors was played at Crosley Field, in Cincinnati, Ohio, even though J.L. Wilkinson, owner of the Kansas City Monarchs, had gambled his life savings back in 1929 to put on the first night ball game in Lawrence, Kansas in March 1930.

Amid this continued backdrop of violence and hatred, Byron found solace in baseball, his family, and teaching. He had been going home in the summers, while at Wiley, to play summer baseball for the Dubisson Tigers. During the summer of 1936, while playing a game in Shreveport a Kansas City Monarch scout spotted the slick fielding shortstop and offered him a contract.

"I was still a homeboy. Christine and I were getting serious, I was teaching school and coaching, and I just wasn't interested in moving to Kansas City...so I didn't take their offer. I loved being back in Little Rock, loved teaching and coaching, although the coaching was starting to wear on me. It was giving me headaches. I was trying to do too much."

In fact Byron would give up coaching football at Dunbar and just stick to teaching science. "I loved butterflies and the Monarch was my favorite, but there was one story I used to love telling my students, and I think every kid who had science from me heard this story. I'd tell them that when I was a kid growing up I'd take my dog for walks in the woods. One day I came across two snakes fighting. Each had the other one by the tail and was swallowing it. I stood there and watched them slowly swallow each other. Suddenly, my dog jumped and ran between my legs. It startled me and I looked away. When I turned around to watch the snakes again, they were gone...they'd eaten each other completely up. I'd stop for a second, look at the kids, then start laughing, then they knew I was kidding."

The year 1936 would end about the way it started, teaching, playing baseball in the summer, and of course, Christine. The Monarchs were still after him, and with the prodding and encouragement of his dad, he would relent in 1937.

"The Monarchs were still after me. They'd sent me a contract and letter. You didn't make much back then, sometimes we didn't get paid at all. We played the game 'cause we loved it. I still didn't want to go, but my dad said, 'You have a brother and sister in Kansas City, you can stay with them, and if you don't like it you can come home.' I thought about it a couple of days and decided he was right."

Byron hadn't been able to join the Monarchs during the spring, because he was teaching school. So when summer rolled around, it was time to leave. While Byron was riding the train from Little Rock to Kansas City, Satchel Paige was threatening to put an end to the Negro Leagues by leading a walkout of the most prominent players. They all headed south to the Dominican Republic for what they hoped was better treatment and more money. The money they got, especially Satch - $30,000, but the treatment, that was a different story.

Paige and his band of malcontents played for Ciudad Trujillo, a team owned and controlled by dictator Rafael Trujillo, who took baseball, well, to say serious would be putting it mildly. They barely escaped losing the series to San Pedro de Macoris, which meant they barely escaped losing their lives. Trujillo had his army surround the field during the last game, and Paige knew if they didn't win, they'd never be allowed to leave. They won, barely 6-5, with Satch striking out five of the last six batters. He would later tell Byron, "You could see Trujillo lining up his army. They began to look like a firing squad."

Years later he could laugh about it, Byron said, but not at the time.

7

Leaving home can be chancy. Some people want to, others have to, but for Byron, it was simply a new world, a world of uncertainty. In Little Rock he knew what he had, the security, family, Christine. But now…well, who knew? A new team, a great team, a new city, new teammates. As the train sped along the track, all those thoughts rushed through his mind. Those words his dad had told him tumbled over and over in his head: "If you don't like it you can come back home." Nice, sentimental, but he knew deep down that was not an option. He loved baseball, and he was going to get to play for the best, but there was still that little boy in him that wanted to be safe.

"When the train got to Kansas City, instead of going to the ballpark, I went straight to my sister Helen's house. It was the same house I ran away from after my mom died. I was twenty-six now and it seemed...nicer. I don't know what I was thinking, I guess I figured I'd just stay there, you know, go to the ballpark, later."

His brother Louis knew he was coming and that he was supposed to be at the field. The game had already started, and the Monarchs were expecting this smooth-fielding shortstop from Little Rock. His brother was also waiting at the ballpark, and when Byron didn't show up, he told the team, "I bet I know where that boy is."

"Sure nuff, here came Louis, grabbed me and off we went to the ballpark. The Monarchs were playing the Birmingham Black Barons and they were in the third or fourth inning. The Monarchs were ahead. Somebody handed me a uniform, I changed in the dugout and sat down. Then the owner, J.L.Wilkinson, walked into the dugout, came over to me, said, 'I know you have been traveling all night, but this would be a good time to try you.' Now, the Monarchs had a man named Willard Brown playing shortstop, I had played against him when he was playing with the Monroe Monarchs in 1934. One of his nicknames was Home Run Brown, he could hit a ton."

Byron was being asked to replace, at shortstop, one of the premier sluggers in black baseball. Willard would, in fact, be the foremost home-run hitter in the decade of the 1940s in the Negro Leagues. He loved the game and in the summers would play in Puerto Rico, where he was nicknamed "Esse Hombre", and had a lifetime .350 batting average. Although a dominant player in the Negro Leagues, his brief stint in the Majors was less than successful. Not given time to adjust to big league white baseball he hit .179 with one home run while playing with the St. Louis Browns in 1947. The one home run he hit was the first ever hit in the American League by a black player. He had borrowed the bat from another player on the team. Rather than let Willard use the bat again, the teammate broke it. His career ran from 1935 to 1950. He retired and settled in Houston and was hospitalized in 1989 with Alzheimer's Disease.

"My shoes cost me $15 and I was playing with a small stiff glove," Byron said. "The catcher for the Monarchs was Frank Duncan. He took a look at my glove and said, 'Where'd you get that? You better get yourself a glove, boy.' It might have been small and stiff, but it had always worked. I went in the game, turned a double play and the fans went wild. The manager, Andy Cooper, greeted me as I came off the field and said, 'You have a job if you want it.' Then he went over to Willard and told him he was moving him to the outfield. My first game...I'll never forget it."

What Byron didn't know was that the Monarchs

had been looking for a shortstop for over a year. Brown was the personification of a power hitter and fleet of foot. But being swift doesn't necessarily make for a great shortstop, where the premium is on fast hands and quick feet, Byron's greatest assets, along with his shotgun arm.

At second the Monarchs had arguably the best second sacker in baseball, Newt Allen. Newton Henry Allen (Newt) played a little over 20 years, mostly with the Kansas City Monarchs. He played some third base, a little outfield, and even managed them for a while in 1941. But his main and best position was second base. He was slick-fielding, had great range and could turn the double play as smooth as silk. For the two years Byron played shortstop for the Monarchs, Newt was his keystone combination partner. They would become fast friends. Newt finished his career with the Monarchs in 1944, then managed the Indianapolis Clowns in 1947, his last year in organized baseball. He retired in Kansas City and became involved in Democratic politics.

"That first season we were playing a game in Chicago against the Chicago American Giants. They had a big, mean first baseman named Ed Young. He had a reputation of...well, coming after you. Here I was 5'8" and 145 pounds soaking wet. He had to be over six feet tall and two hundred pounds (he was actually 6'2' and weighed 210 lbs.). Well, anyway, he gets a hit and is on at first base. The next hitter grounds the ball to Newt and we turn a nice smooth double play. "Big" Young is out by ten feet. I'm on my way back to short, when he comes around the bag and tries to spike me. I looked up at him, he grinned at me and ran off the field. Newt saw it, 'Mex, you better get tough, don't be takin' that stuff, 'cause they'll run you out of the league.' A couple of innings go by and sure nuff, Young's on first again. The ball's hit to Newt, I came across the bag and fired it to first base, right at Young's head. He ducked just in time, his hat flew off and that ball went into his hat and on to first base...double play!

"That night some of us were eating at a local diner, when who appeared in the doorway..."Big" Young. He was with a couple teammates. He stood in the door, looked around and saw me sitting in the back. Here he came right at me. He looked even bigger and meaner walking toward me. I looked down at the table, all I had was a spoon and fork to defend myself. I figured I was going to get pounded. I thought, well, he might be bigger and stronger, but I know I'm faster, and he ain't goin' to pound me if he can't catch me. Anyway, he walked up to the table, I looked up, he stared down, I grabbed my spoon and fork, and I remember thinking, this is goin' to be a long season if I have to go through this all the time. He looked at me real surly like, then said, 'Hi Mex,' then turned around and walked off. A few minutes went by before I could let go of the fork and spoon. I told Newt about it and he said, 'You just gettin' their respect Mex.' That was really the last time I had that kind of trouble on the field, but I'll never forget "Big" Ed Young and that flyin' hat."

Byron was an outstanding fielder, maybe the best of his time. One of his compatriots in later years said, "He was the Oz before the Oz, referring to Ozzie Smith. He was quick, fast, and could steal bases with the best of them. Could bunt well, but struggled at hitting for average.

"I just couldn't hit that curve ball," Byron said half joking. "Chicago had this pitcher, Trent [Ted Trent] and he had the best curve ball I'd ever seen. In one game against them he struck me out every time up, all curve balls. I never could hit that man."

Ted Trent was a tall, lanky right-hander with a reputation for throwing maybe the best "Big" breaker in the Negro Leagues. He liked to say he had three curves, the long curve, the short curve and the shorter curve. He had a good fastball and a drop pitch, but what made all this work, was his great control. He had a twelve-year career in black ball finishing up with the Chicago American Giants in 1939. He lived hard and played hard, and four years after retiring, he contracted tuberculosis and died shortly after his fortieth birthday in 1944.

"Trent had the best curve ball, but I had trouble hitting everybody's curve. One of my favorites on the Monarchs was Bullet Rogan. He was an old veteran and hated seeing me whiff on that curve ball. He told me, 'If you can hit Trent, then you got it.' He'd meet me before games and throw me curve after curve. He had me open my stance a little too, so I could see the ball better. It worked, 'cause not soon after we were playing Chicago again, facing Trent. He tried spinning one on me, and I hit it off the right field fence. After that, well, I didn't hit the curve great, but I didn't strike out on it all the time either."

Wilbur (Bullet) Rogan had a long and distinguished career in the Negro Leagues. He pitched, played infield, and outfield, and managed. He had a tremendous fastball, good curve, and great control. "He was a gentleman, a good family man," Byron recalled. His last two years in baseball were Byron's first two years with the Monarchs. While playing baseball in the service, from 1911 to 1919, he was discovered by Casey Stengel, who recommended him to J.L. Wilkinson, the eventual owner of the Monarchs. Jocko Conlan, who some consider the greatest umpire that ever lived, and who used to play against Negro

Leaguers before starting his adjudicator career, once stated he thought Bullet threw harder than Satchel Paige. Once he was through playing and managing, he followed Jocko into the world of umpiring, doing so in the Negro American League for a few years. He then moved permanently to Kansas City and worked for the post office. Byron stayed in touch with him until the mid-1960s.

"We were having a reunion there in Kansas City and I asked where Bullet was. Somebody told me he was in a retirement home on the edge of town. I asked around and found out which one. I went out there, but they wouldn't let me in to see him. One of the security men, told me to come back that night and he'd let me in. I went back that night and he took me up to Bullet's room. It was sorta dark and he was lying on a bed in the corner of the room. I walked up and put my hand on his shoulder, he kinda rolled over. He looked so sick, it made me sick. I said, 'Bullet, it's me.' He tried to look up at me, but I don't think he could see anymore. I said it again. He turned toward me and said, 'Mex, is that you?' Here was a man who'd been so good, so strong, I didn't know what to do. The place he was staying in wasn't very nice, so I tried to get some other guys, so we could raise some money and move him to a better place. It never happened, and he died there in 1967. He will always be someone I think kindly of, and wish I could have done more for."

Byron struggled with breaking pitches, but fastballs, well, that was another story. Whether it was Bob Feller or Willie Foster, getting the heater by Byron was next to impossible. Byron faced Feller several times over his career when Feller and his All-Stars would barnstorm. When asked if he could hit Feller's fastball, Byron would smile and say, "He couldn't get it by me." One of the hardest throwers in black ball was William (Willie) Foster, half-brother of the famous Rube Foster. This gangly lefthander could bring the heat. "Foster was a terror," Byron said grinning. "But I could hit that man. It would make him so angry. I don't care how hard he threw it...I hit it!"

Willie Foster played from 1923 to 1938. Although half-brother of the founder of the Negro National League, Rube Foster hindered his career early on, which lingered with Willie the rest of his life. He eventually played for Rube with the Chicago American Giants. He had a sterling career and was well respected. While playing ball, he pursued his education, getting his degree and upon retiring from baseball he became the dean of men and baseball coach at Alcorn State College in Mississippi. He held this position until shortly before his death in 1978.

Byron's first year with the Monarchs, 1937, they won the pennant. They'd been playing independent ball up until that year. This was their first year in the

Negro American League, and over the next six seasons they would win five pennants. "That first season was pretty interesting. All the travel, different cities, fields, bigger crowds and playing with and against the best ballplayers in the world." However interesting for Byron, the season was even more attention-grabbing for the league. Heretofore Latin American countries had limited their American baseball activities to winter ball. Now, however, they had expanded into summer ball. The first and most dramatically affected was black ball. Led by Satchel Paige, many departed for Puerto Rico and the Dominican Republic. After that harrowing experience in the Dominican Republic, the players returned in the fall of 1937. Having been banned from the league, they formed their own touring all-star team called the Trujillo All-Stars hoping to cash in on their aforementioned notoriety. All would be resolved, albeit with hard feelings, by the spring of 1938. This would also commence Byron's greatest season in baseball.

8

His first year with the Monarchs, they'd won the pennant, then beaten the Chicago American Giants four out of five games to win the league crown. Byron felt as though he'd been a key component of it, although he'd only been with them for part of the season. Still and all, he'd contributed, made an impression, been successful.

The year 1938 would also be a significant year for Byron off the field. After courting Christine for several years, they decided to get married. While Byron was off playing baseball, Christine had moved to Danville, Arkansas, where she was born, and had gotten a job teaching. She'd found out about the job through the WPA and wound up teaching her cousins. After one year there, she moved to Lonoke, Arkansas and got another teaching job. As the Monarchs motored their way south, Byron took a small detour, went to Lonoke, picked up Christine, went to the courthouse and they got married. At the end of the school year she moved back to Little Rock and started teaching at Stephens Elementary. This then was the ceremonial beginning of a life-long love affair.

While the Monarchs wouldn't win the pennant in 1938, Byron would excel. It would be his most successful season as a pro. He was more settled now, used to the routine. The ROUTINE, however, in Negro League ball was anything but. Traveling in cars and buses or on an occasional train were the only ways to get from city to city and ballpark to ballpark. They ate on the move and sometimes would have to sleep in the cars or on the ball field. The only place to clean up was in the bathrooms, or as in most instances, not at all.

"When I was with the Little Rock Stars, we'd get paid $50 or $60 a month, and it wasn't much more with the Monarchs. We had trouble getting food. But what we could always find was baloney, cheese and crackers. That was real popular back then...I guess 'cause it was easy to get. Wilkie always took care of us though. He was one of the finest men, black, white or whatever, that I ever met. We all loved him."

J. Leslie Wilkinson (Wilkie) was born in Perry, Iowa, in 1874. His father was the president of Algona Normal College. He pitched a little baseball as a kid, and as a young man, in and around Iowa for various pro and semipro teams, all under the assumed name of Joe Green. He later started playing with the Hopkins Brothers Sporting Goods Store team, and when the manager vanished with all the money, his teammates voted him in as manager. He would stay in management the rest of his baseball days. Always the innovator, he formed the All Nations team, which provided a broad spectrum of entertainment beyond baseball. The team came accompanied by a wrestling team and an orchestra. By 1915, Wilkinson moved the All Nations team from Des Moines to Kansas City, and by 1920, they became the Monarchs. He had a reputation for being diplomatic, easygoing and unassuming. He was respected and liked by those playing for him as well as those playing against him. After twenty-eight years, sick and almost blind, he sold his remaining half interest in the Monarchs to Tom Baird. Black sportswriters around the country elegized, "Negro baseball...lost one of its finest and smartest men." He'd always been a class act, whether dealing with his players or the fans. He'd been the first owner in all of baseball to use lights and play night games. His love of the game was unquestioned. He died August 21, 1964 in Kansas City, Missouri.

"We played a lot of games," Byron remembered. "A league game in the afternoon, then a quick trip to another town and a barnstorming game that night. Sometimes we'd play a double header in the morning and then another one at twilight. It wasn't unusual for our team to rack up almost 250 games a season." By 1938, Byron had given up teaching and was devoting his full time to his baseball career.

This kind of wear and tear on their bodies and psyches eventually took its toll on all of them, some more than others, some sooner than others. Not only were the travel conditions brutal, but once they got where they were going hospitality was, shall we say, less than cordial.

"One night we'd played a game in Jackson, Mississippi. After the game we were tired and hungry. We went back to the hotel, cleaned up and three or four of us were gonna go get something to eat. When we came out the front door of the hotel there were two big white policemen standing there. They took one look at us, stopped us, said, 'Boy, where do you think you're goin'?' They wouldn't let us leave to get something to eat. We had to go back up to our rooms. We called Wilkie and told him he'd better come over. It was kind of late, and he showed up in his pajamas. He took those policemen aside, said something to them, and sure enough we got to go out and eat."

Finding a place to stay, other than in the car or on the field, not to speak of places to eat, other than gas stations, would be a constant perplexity and source of irritation for all black ballplayers. "We put up with it because we loved the game. There were games we never got paid for, it was the love of the game," Byron said proudly. "We stayed away from the South because of the way we were treated. It wasn't as bad in the North or Midwest, and in Canada we could go everywhere, could eat anywhere...and most of the fans were white!"

While Byron and the Monarchs were now playing in the Negro American League, Satchel Paige and his Trujillo All-Stars were barnstorming through the Midwest late in the summer of 1937. By the time they entered the Denver Post tournament they were now known as the Satchel Paige All-Stars, and due to their namesake's legendary star power, were outdrawing the other Negro League teams and their postseason extravaganzas. This deflected attention, as well as decreased ticket receipts, motivated the power brokers in black baseball to rethink their lifetime bans on the expatriated players.

They scheduled a series of games between the Negro National League Homestead Grays and an All-Star squad of players from the Negro American League. The final game took place in New York's Polo Grounds before 22,500 boisterous fans. Johnny Taylor matched scoreless innings with Paige until the eighth when Paige gave up a two-run homer to Jim West. Taylor retired George Scales, Spoony Palm, and Cool Papa Bell in the top of the ninth to preserve his mesmerizing no-hitter. The black press would call it the "greatest game ever played." Beyond this, it opened the door for the ostracized players to return to the league in time for the 1938 season.

While it would not be the typical winning season for the Monarchs, it would be a sterling season for Byron. Although an average hitter, he could bunt with the best of them and with his outstanding speed on the base paths was in the upper echelon in stolen bases and runs scored. In the field he was arguably the best shortstop during that 1938 season. He had unmatched range, soft, quick hands and a lightning bolt arm. His excellent play and outstanding talent would be rewarded with a starting berth in the East-West All-Star game.

The East-West All-Star game was the pinnacle of the season, drawing more fans and attention than their version of the World Series or any other event in black baseball. Finances being what they were in the Negro Leagues - desperate - the owners decided to schedule a second All-Star game during the 1938 season. Fans always picked the teams, so to justify a second game the owners issued a statement saying the fans hadn't picked the best players for the game in Chicago. This time the sportswriters would pick the teams, thereby assuring everyone the best players would be involved. The game would be played in New York. The true basis and certainty of this decision was...MONEY!

Given the acknowledgement and magnitude of the game, the players would and did play for nothing. Payment came in the form of honor. "I'd have to say my biggest thrill was the first time I went to the East- West classic," stated Jesse Williams of the Monarchs. In fact, during the 1930s, the players received no remuneration for participating in the game. As one sportswriter put it, "The average colored player has been interested more or less in his salary and what it would be, but now they are all trying to make the East – West classic." Byron was no exception. "That was without doubt the high point of my career. Getting to play with the best players in the world. I'll never forget it."

The receipts for the All-Star game in Chicago were $27,000, from which each owner collected $900. The owners of Comiskey Park, however, were the real winners as they received 20 to 25 percent of the gate proceeds for use of the stadium as well as monies for use of dressing rooms and dugouts. There would be no second All-Star game in New York in 1938. Robert Jackson, president of the Negro American League, refused to sanction the game and stated he would fine every player who participated twenty-five dollars. Players protested in vain. In 1939, however, both the Negro American League and Negro National League did authorize a second All-Star game in New York. The West changed the line-up from the Chicago game, but the East used the same team. Only twenty thousand people showed up. That was the first, and last of doubling up on All-Star games.

Byron went one for four in the 1938 All-Star game, getting a single in his first at bat. The day of the game Turkey Stearns, a teammate and a man known for being frugal with his equipment, especially his bats, loaned one to Byron. "Mex, if you get a hit you can keep the bat; if you don't, bring me back my bat." The West won the game 5-4. Byron would later donate that bat to the Negro Leagues Baseball Museum in Kansas City, Missouri.

In the burgeoning metropolis of New York, writer and anthropologist Zora Neale Hurston's book of Negro folklore, *Tell My Horse*, was published. Through her field research in Jamaica and Haiti she tracked how African stories survived the diaspora in the Americas. Playwright Thornton Wilder premiered his drama, *Our Town*, on Broadway. It became the most performed American play of the century, and at Carnegie Hall, John Hammond, a young record producer and resolute anti-segregationist, produced *"Spirituals to Swing."* It brought boogie-woogie, gospel, and jazz artists of the future to mainstream audiences. Hammond would discover such musical luminaries as Billie Holiday, Count Basie, Benny Goodman, Aretha Franklin, George Benson, and Bruce Springsteen.

9

"I was beat. I knew it. There was no place to turn. I was a big man who was just falling into that old land, where nobody knows you." - Satchel Paige, 1939.

After years and years of use and abuse, his arm had died, and with it his reputation, at least as a pitcher. Satch had not only used up his arm, but his fragile relationship with black baseball. Showing up late for games, or not showing up at all. Breaking contracts, demanding and getting the bulk of receipts, at the expense of teammates. He was, without doubt, the biggest name in the game, but some felt he was also the biggest jerk. Now, with nowhere to turn, he felt deserted.

Baseball had been his one and only livelihood. It's what defined him as an athlete, a celebrity, and a man. Oh, he had other interests, money, women, guns, and cameras, but baseball, that was the engine that drove Satchel's train. He'd grown up in Mobile, Alabama...and didn't want to go back. "It'd been a long time since I'd thought about having nothing, about how it was to grow up in Mobile," he said thinking back. "Ten years can make for a lot of forgetting. Now I started remembering. I didn't want to go back, but baseball was the only thing that'd keep me away."

Satch turned to the only man he hadn't directly or indirectly offended in baseball, J.L. Wilkinson. J.L. was a man of compassion, a man of fairness, but he was also a great promoter. He knew Satch was damaged goods and a troubled man. He wanted to reach out to the distressed side of Satchel's inner being, but he also saw potential, as in gate attendance. Wilkinson not only dealt with his players evenhandedly, which in turn provided him with great teams, but he was a master of bally-hoo. Music, wrestlers, the first to use lights and originate night baseball. Now, here before him, he had the single most flamboyant and popular player in Negro baseball, an orbiting soul looking for a soft place to land. Where better than the Monarchs, with a man he trusted?

Paige called Wilkinson in the spring of 1939. "My arm won't do any throwin'," he told Wilkinson. But there was far more here than the condition of Satch's arm. There was his name, his legend, and the mere magic of seeing the tall, lanky righthander on the field. It was this charismatic presence J.L. would capitalize on.

How better to make the most of this unique circumstance than to name a team after the myth? They would be known as the Satchel Paige All-Stars, and Byron "Mex" Johnson would be their shortstop.

To avoid interlopers from other teams, Wilkinson let it be known Paige was indeed hurt. His signing was more an act of benevolence than shrewd baseball acumen. To this end he used the news media to foster the scheme. On March 11, the *Kansas City Call* reported, as per J.L.'s instructions, "The great one owned a wing that was as dead as a new bride's biscuit. Satch's great flipper just wouldn't work any more. It was at that time that Wilkinson toyed with the idea of employing Satch, who was nursing the once-poisonous paw in pathetic pity."

Through the press Wilkinson would constantly maneuver Paige's resurgent career. With Paige unable to throw like the Satch of old, J.L. created interest by manufacturing...well, enhancing, what were heretofore, unknown facts. His skywriters claimed, "Paige is a good hitter. He can play first base.... His total batting average is .343 for all games he has worked in." All geared to reconstruct what was assumed to be a fading fable. But there was a subtext to this. J.L. Wilkinson also wanted it to be known Satchel Paige was his. Although there had been little, if any, interest expressed by other owners, if Paige somehow made a miraculous recovery, you could take it to the bank they'd come a calling. Even though they had all poor-mouthed him, they also knew he was still the biggest draw in the game. Byron remembered it well. "We played all through Kansas and Missouri and Illinois and, boy, the people really turned out to see him."

On April 21, the *Kansas City Call* ran a headline, "SATCHEL PAIGE JOINS KANSAS CITY MONARCHS." With Satch unable to throw, Wilkinson had no intention of putting him on the established Monarch team. The way to get the most out of Paige's reputation was to give him his own team. The actual name was the Travelers, a team Wilkinson made up of young players looking to make the big club, men on the down side of their careers, and men with a specific purpose for being there. Byron was one of these men, the point men.

To further distance this team from the owners in the Negro American League and Negro National League, he put his brother Lee in charge, which established a pseudo separation between the big club and the Travelers. Newt Joseph, who'd had a long distinguished career with the Monarchs as a third baseman, managed the team. Now forty years old, seasoned in the ways of black baseball, liked and respected by his fellow players, Joseph was the best choice to head up this eclectic bunch.

Walter Newton (Newt) Joseph was born in Montgomery, Alabama in 1899, but reared in Muskogee, Oklahoma. He'd started out as a pitcher and catcher, but wound up as a third baseman. Hitchhiking to Kansas City in the early 1920s, he'd demanded a uniform from the Monarchs and was given one as a gag. With hustle, hard work, and a sometimes-nasty attitude, he made the most of his modest talents, becoming a fixture with the Monarchs from 1922 to 1935. Wilkinson then made him the manager of the Paige All-Stars. Upon retiring from baseball, he opened a taxicab stand in Kansas City. He died in 1953, in Kansas City, from tuberculosis.

"I always liked Newt," Byron recalled. "He was fair and kept us together...and he could handle Satch, which wasn't easy. Satch kinda had his own way of doin' things, but Newt always seemed okay with it."

There were a number of young players needing seasoning, but there were some old vets – they were the drawing cards, along with, of course, Satch. They had George Giles at first, pitchers Big Train Jackson and John Marcum.

James Thomas (Cool Papa) Bell. Long and lean, his ability to run the base paths was legendary. When Jesse Owens returned from the Olympics in 1936, Gus Greenlee, a mogul in Negro League ball, hired him to race against racehorses around the bases, and occasionally another ballplayer. He'd give them a ten-yard head start and still beat them. Cool Papa was another matter however, "I don't ever remember him racing Cool Papa," recalled teammate Buck O'Neil. "I don't think he wanted to take the chance. Boy, that would have been something. I'll say this, going from first to home, Jesse wouldn't have beaten Cool Papa. He was the fastest man I ever saw."

Bell was arguably the fastest man to play the game. He once stole 175 bases in just under 200 games. "If he bunts and it bounces twice, put it in your pocket, " said "Double Duty" Radcliffe, one of the most versatile players to ever play the game. On numerous occasions Radcliffe was known to pitch one game of a double header and catch the second and due to this unique ability was given the name "Double Duty" by the famous sportswriter/playwright Damon Runyon.

"If he (Bell) hits one back to the pitcher, everyone yelled, 'Hurry!'" claimed Jimmy Crutchfield, a spunky little outfielder who played 15 years in the Negro Leagues.

Some, obviously stretching the truth, even claim they saw him hit a ball up the middle, then was called out when HIT by his own-batted ball while sliding into second. Cool Papa Bell was truly one of the high profile stars of the Negro Leagues. He closed his career with a lifetime batting average of .341 after a quarter century in black baseball. Further evidence of his brilliance was his .391 average in exhibition games against major leaguers. Late in his career he declined an offer from the St. Louis Browns, but did accept a position as a part time scout with the organization, until they moved to Baltimore in 1954. When his baseball days were over, he worked as a custodian and night security officer at the St. Louis City Hall, retiring in 1970. He was honored for his magnificent baseball career in 1974, with his induction into the National Baseball Hall of Fame. He died in 1991 in St. Louis, Missouri.

"I knew who he was, I'd heard all about him," Byron remembered. "Our manager told me, 'Now, when Cool Papa comes up, you move way in, cause it's the only way you have a chance.' So the first time I played against him he hits the ball up the middle into center. I go out to get the throw in and when I turn around he's on third. I thought, no way he's that fast. His next time up he hits one by second base into the outfield, so I watch him, sure nuff, he cuts in front of second and straight over to third. I went over to him standing on third and said, 'Hey,' he looked at me and said, 'Ya saw me huh.' Later he told me, 'We only got two umpires and when the ball's hit into the outfield, that guy goes out to watch the ball. They don't watch me, so...' Even with him cuttin' the base-paths he was the fastest man I ever saw."

It was a different story with Josh Gibson, the personification of clout. Byron's first encounter with the powerful Gibson was a lesson, not in quickness, but self defense. "They told me to back up when Josh Gibson came to the plate. I didn't believe them. I was pretty cocky and sure of myself. Well, Josh hit a ball so hard at me, it was on me before I could get my glove down. It bounced once and hit me in the leg. Man, did that sucker hurt! I could see the marks of the stitches from the ball on my leg two weeks later."

With his moniker on the team, Satch was reborn. "I'd been dead. Now I was alive again." Paige remembered. "I didn't have my arm, but I didn't even think of that. I had me a piece of work." As the team barnstormed through the Northwest, Midwest, and California, Paige was not only the draw, but also a coach, and a man still striving for equality. "When Satchel Paige had his All-Stars they wouldn't play in a town if they couldn't lodge there," recalled Jack Marshall of the Chicago American Giants. "Wilkinson owned the ball club, and if Satchel Paige couldn't sleep where they played or eat where they played, they wouldn't play there. He'd just tell the Chamber of Commerce, no soap. They were warned beforehand, so they didn't have any trouble; the Chamber of Commerce made the arrangements."

Byron, along with the other players, had no idea if or how badly Satch's arm was hurt. They would only find that out after the fact. Wilkinson had purpose in connecting Byron with Satchel. Because of Byron's college degree and easy manner, J.L. figured Byron could keep Satchel out of trouble...at least for the most part.

"Mr. Wilkinson asked me directly to stay with Satchel. He knew what a crazy son of a gun he was and figured I could keep him on the straight and narrow. He told me, 'Mex, you stay with him. Don't let him out of your sight,' which I did for a while. I couldn't ride with him though, his drivin' was too fast. I figured I wasn't goin' to live through it, so I stopped riding with him and started riding with Lee (Mr. Wilkinson's brother)."

"We were sittin' on the porch of this hotel in Bismarck (North Dakota). The mayor in Bismarck loved Satch, he could get anything he wanted there. Satch had bought one of these new fangled cameras that you could stand up on a tripod. He's gonna take a picture of us. There's me, Newt, and Satch is gonna set the timing on the camera and run back in the picture.

As he's settin' the camera up he sees this pretty woman walkin' up the street toward us. Now, if there's one thing Satch liked as much as guns and cameras, it was women. So he stops, goes over and talks to her a minute, then brings her back, steps in front of the camera with her and takes their picture. We looked like shadows in the background. When we asked him what he was doin', he said, 'I'll get a picture with anyone I want.'" I'll never forget it...that was Satch."

One of the other point men for Wilkinson was Frank "Jewbaby" Floyd, the longtime trainer of the Monarchs. His job was to rehabilitate Satchel's valuable wing. He'd rub it with liniments, and oils and wrap it in hot towels. " 'Cause he didn't go to no doctor for it," Buck O'Neil recalled. "What happened was, Jewbaby went out on the road with Satchel. He worked on that arm, just rubbin' it with different things. It couldn't have been too serious, 'cause Satchel went out there and pitched and the arm came around and he came right back. "The doctors said it was serious, and for most guys that woulda been it. But the doctors didn't know Satchel."

"Jewbaby was a tall drink of water," Byron said. "He might have been taller than Satch, maybe 6'4" or so. He was always rubbin' stuff on Satch's arm. I never knew what it was, but it must a worked. He was throwin' like the old Satch, before long."

As the *Pittsburgh Courier* reported, "Jewbaby cuddles and baby's that bronze slingshot Satchel carries around on the right side of his anatomy for an arm."

Byron, like everyone else on the team, wasn't really sure how bad Satch's arm was, or when it began to recover. "He wasn't throwin' like the old Satch, but he was still getting' people out, and the fans loved to watch him, no matter what he was doin'."

Wilkinson was astounded that this backup barnstorming team was outdrawing the Monarchs: more fans, more press coverage, generally more attention. Although the All-Stars were sometimes difficult to locate, the press always seemed to find them. This convergence of notoriety and currency put Wilkinson in a quandary. He wanted Satchel Paige back on the Monarchs. Beyond the fact he was...well, Satchel Paige, his arm was steadily improving and Byron and the rest of the All-Stars were starting to see the notorious gunslinger return to form incinerating hitters with his flame-throwing fastball.

"I was in Toledo and my season was over," remembered Connie Johnson, who played that '39 season with the Toledo Crawfords. " I heard Satchel was coming to town so I stayed over a week to see him. I'd never seen him before, but my uncle used to talk about him like in 1926, how great he was and all that. So I had to go see him.

"They was playing the Toledo Mudhens, which was a white team, a Triple-A farm team and the ballpark was jes packed, and mostly with white people, 'cause everybody heard of him. And so I'm up there in the grandstand and I'm watchin' Satchel warm up and it's like...there was a team back then called the Clowns and they had a little show they would put on before games called 'shadowball,' they'd make like they were throwin' the ball but they didn't. So the first man Satchel pitched to, I thought he was playin' shadowball, 'Cuz I didn't see the ball."

With his heater back, Satchel found his other pitches were even more effective, i.e. the famous Hesitation Pitch. "See, he was using it as a change of pace, 'cause he didn't have a curveball. I don't ever remember him throwin' no curve," Byron declared. "And when he did this with men on, he'd be lookin' around while he did that hesitatin', and it was really a balk. He balked a lot of times only they didn't call it. Maybe they were told not to call it, or else they were lettin' him get away with it 'cause of who he was. But them runners had to hold up, and they couldn't score when they should have."

As Wilkinson feared, once the word got out Paige's arm was back, the previously acrimonious owners had a newfound interest. By the spring of 1940, Satchel Paige...the old, new version would be a sizzling issue.

In 1939, the film *Gone With the Wind* was released dealing with the Civil War and Reconstruction, depicting slaves as loyal and docile. Hattie McDaniel became the first African American to receive an Oscar for her role as Mammy in the film. It was the last one for the next 25 years.

Jazz singer Billie Holiday recorded *"Strange Fruit,"* a song about the lynching of blacks in the South.

The World's Fair began in New York with the theme; *"Building the World of Tomorrow,"* while World War II began in Europe as Hitler invaded Poland.

10

When 1939 came to an end, at least the baseball season, Byron was tired. He'd seen more of North America than he thought possible, and had been forced to do it in cars, buses, and an occasional train.

"The travel just wore us out." Byron proclaimed. "We'd play a game, couldn't clean up, and then have to travel...sometimes 200 miles, and play again. Sometimes the only sleep we could get was in the car. It was tough, and we sure didn't do it for the money. We did it 'cause we loved the game."

They had to; there were no other redeeming features. There was no fame or fortune for these men. In fact, it was quite the opposite. The only man who courted either was Satchel Paige. Oh, there were a few who rode Paige's coattails, like Josh Gibson, Buck Leonard, and Cool Papa Bell, but none attained the stature of Satch. It wasn't because they didn't have the talent...they did. Cool Papa Bell may have been the fastest man to ever play the game and Josh Gibson was certainly one of the great homerun hitters of all time, but no one had the flamboyance and pure audacity that Paige had. Whether in black or white baseball, he was one of a kind.

The majority of the players, however, were like Byron, excellent ballplayers, but no one knew anything about them outside of black baseball. They did have one thing going for them however: education. In 1940 over half the Negro league players had some college. This was not the case in the white Major Leagues. Byron had a degree, and in the back of his mind, he knew he would teach one day. Baseball was his love, but would not be his lifelong vocation. In fact, in the off-season he went back to Little Rock to teach.

"I loved biology and loved teaching it. Plus, although Christine always supported what I did, we missed each other. I had a family, and it was hard being away."

But away he was again in 1940. Back on the road, traveling with Satch and his All-Stars. Byron had gotten used to Paige's idiosyncrasies, at least for the most part. He tried riding with him again, but it was just too...DANGEROUS! "I don't know what it was with

Lizzie Golden Johnson   Joseph Simeon Johnson

Sadie Johnson Pendleton
on her wedding day

The Johnson siblings at the funeral of their father -
December 1952
Top: Earl, Louis, Mark, Byron
Bottom: Clayborn, Mabel, Horatius, Helen
(Sadie had died in 1936.)

Byron Johnson's football team when he played at
Dunbar High School in Little Rock, Arkansas, 1929.

Byron's nickname was "Mex". He's standing on the right.

The Dubisson Tigers' semi-pro baseball team, 1936.
Byron is top row center.

1939 Kansas City Monarchs
Byron Johnson is front row, far left.
Manager Newt Joseph is front row, far right.

The Shortstop
on the road with
the Satchel Paige
All Stars, 1940

While traveling
with the
Satchel Paige
All Stars.
Washington,
1940

Byron Johnson's Army photo,
World War II

Byron,
as a young man

Christine,
as a young
woman

Byron and Christine Johnson

Byron Johnson coming to see Kansas City Monarch teammate, the great Satchel Paige, play in Denver.

Christine and Byron's son, Joseph Byron Johnson at 11 years of age.

Byron Johnson playing with the Post Office softball team in Denver. Byron is kneeling next to the end on the right.

Byron Johnson
in front of Dunbar
High School sign.
Little Rock, Arkansas,
1999

Byron with Baseball historian Jay Sanford, 2000

Byron with teammate Buck O'Neil, 2000

Byron with Don Baylor and daughter Jackie at
Coors Field before throwing out the first pitch, 2000.

Byron speaking at the Byron and Christine Johnson
Lecture/Discussion Series, 2000.

Byron Johnson,
2000

Carlotta Walls LaNier representing Byron
when he was inducted as an Honorary Member of the
Saskatchewan Baseball Hall of Fame in Canada, 2004.

The Hitter's Hands of Byron Johnson,
a bronze sculpure created by Raelee Frazier

Three of Byron's great-grandchildren:
Twins Amir and Najah, and Salih.

Byron's 90th birthday party
Byron with niece Carlotta,
granddaughters Lisa and Dominique,
daughter Jackie, and great-granddaughter Desmarae.

Byron Johnson dancing for the family
on Christmas Day, 1995

Byron "Mex" Johnson, 2005

that boy, but when he got to drivin' it was hell on wheels. He got that big old Chrysler up on them mountain roads and he just loved to go fast," Byron said with a grin. "I'd tell him, 'Man I don't wanna ride with you, Satchel.' 'Cause he'd - and he was crazy enough to do this - he would see a deer cut across the highway and follow it. I mean that boy would turn around on the highway or cut across the divider and go after that deer on foot with his rifle. Aw, man, I'd be sittin' there in a big jam-up waitin' for him to come back."

The more the environment changed, the more the circumstances stayed the same for Paige: guns, cameras, and, of course, women. "The women always wanted to be with him, especially the white women," Byron commented. "He had one lady he took up and down the West Coast and up into Canada. That's when he really isolated himself from us."

To say Satchel Paige was an enigma would be an understatement. He was without question the most recognizable, most popular, and certainly the biggest draw in the Negro Leagues. It was these very qualities that allowed him to get away with...well, being Satch. On the field he was flamboyant, overstated, an entertainer. Who else would have his fielders sit down in the field so he could showcase his arsenal of pitches? Apparently, he did this on several occasions, once against white big leaguers in California. He was facing the likes of Frank Demaree, Wally Berger, and Babe Herman. Hearing a racial slur from the stands, he ordered his fielders to sit down. With one down, he then struck out Demaree and Berger. Larry Brown, his catcher that day, verified the story, "Satch, you're the biggest fool ever I've seen in my life. I never saw anybody but you do that with a one run lead." My guess is, one run lead or not, he was the only pitcher in history to orchestrate such an occurrence. The sheer novelty and nerve of it speaks not only to Satchel's talent, but his panache. On another occasion, however, it backfired. Once again he ordered his fielders to sit down, but he failed to strike out the last hitter. Instead the guy hit a shot to center field. Paige, shocked, looked around for his outfielders to help. They sat patiently and told Satch, "Go get it yourself," while the runner circled the bases.

Byron would be witness to this élan on numerous occasions: being part of a squatting infield, hearing Satchel tell the hitters what was coming and they were still unable to do anything about it. All field showmanship, all for the fans, for his opponents and for his teammates. Off the field, however, that was a different matter. At times reclusive, a loner, this is the man Byron would come to know, to the extent Satchel would let him.

"He was a happy man," Byron said smiling. "If he believed in you, he believed in you. He'd drive that big old car and sing; sometimes we'd talk about verses and poems. If I needed something, I could get it from him.

"He'd spend his last penny on a shotgun or a camera, but if I needed a quarter or money for breakfast, he'd give it to me. I used to say to him, 'Satch you sure can throw money around,' but it was his money. Once in Reno (Nevada) he was playin' the quarter slots. He'd used up all his money cause he'd been playin' for over half an hour, so he tried to borrow from me. He played a few more then quit, hadn't won a thing. I walked up dropped one quarter in and hit. I looked at him and said, 'Satch, you just got it ready for me.' He just looked at me and shook his head. He was lots of fun, I liked being around him."

1940 would be the last year Byron would spend with Satchel, and his last year with the Monarchs/All-Stars. As usual the All-Stars started their season in Peoria, Illinois, then ventured north and west from there, through parts of Canada, then into the Mid-west and West. Thousands of miles, thousands of stops, and what seemed like thousands of games.

While touring the West they made a stop in Cheyenne, Wyoming. Known for its cowboys and ranching, Byron was surprised to find racism alive and well in the dusty old cow town. They pulled into a gas station-diner to get gas and food. "I got out of the car and asked about food and the guy said niggers couldn't get any food there. I was shocked because that was the first time I'd heard the word 'nigger' out there, and because I thought I was in a Western city, not like the South. Then Newt and Satch came in and there was a heated conversation and then we left.

"Well, we stopped at that same fillin' station on the way back and they said, 'Yeah, bring 'em in, they can eat here.' See, I think it had gotten around that the guy had refused to serve Satchel Paige, and that you just didn't do that to a star like him."

Byron had been through this before back when he first started playing for the Monarchs on trips down South. Although unsettling, it certainly wasn't unexpected. "Somewhere down South in, I think 1938, we pulled into a filling station to get gas and something to eat. Newt (Allen) started walking toward the station. The man pumping gas said, 'Boy, where do you think you're going?' 'To get something to eat,' Newt said. 'You can't get no food here, jus' gas.' Newt turned around, came back to the cars and said, 'If we can't get no food, then we don't want your gas...take it out.' You shoulda seen that guy sucking that gas back out of those cars. Gas all over him, the street, everywhere, I can still see it."

What had started in June would end in October in games against the American Giants and finish with a game versus the parent club, the Kansas City Monarchs. Satch threw in both games, but was not himself against the Monarchs. The then Monarchs ace, Hilton Smith, would defeat him. Paige removed himself from the game in the fourth inning. The All-Stars took an 11-0 drubbing.

When the season ended, Byron had decided to call it quits. "I just knew we'd never get a chance to play in the majors, and I was tired and scared really of all the travel. I had a family and wanted to go home to my people."

"The last thing Satchel said to me was, 'I don't want to lose you forever.'"

Byron went back to Little Rock, and Satchel went to Mexico to continue his remarkable career. During the off-season, which was rare for Paige, he'd go down to Little Rock and go squirrel hunting with Byron. "I think he came down twice," Byron remembered. Once we were hunting illegally, and the game warden found out and came looking for Satchel. He'd taken off. Two years later he was down again and we were sittin' in the dugout of this ballgame when in walked the game warden, 'It took me two years, but I caught ya,' the warden said smiling. We all had to go pay a fine. Satch thought it was funny...except for the fine."

They'd talk once in a while, but Byron would not see Satchel again until 1972 in Denver at a golf tournament.

One year prior to that, old Satch had been inducted in the Baseball Hall of Fame. He was one of the first three great players from the Negro Leagues to be so honored. In June of 1982, he would die of a heart attack. The legend, the myth, gone; however, his legacy would endure, and, with the long overdue recognition of black baseball, has continued to grow.

As Byron prepared for life after baseball, the United States continued preparations for going to war. Hitler invaded France, and Americans of every color would fight and die in World War II. Byron would train and fight in Europe in a segregated army. "Those were some of the worst days of my life."

11

A man conflicted, right or wrong, good or bad, should I or shouldn't I, this was Byron. He so loved baseball, just playing the game. He loved going in the hole at third, scooping the ball up backhanded, then while pivoting in midair firing across the diamond and getting the runner by two steps, or turning the double play, smooth, quick...the right, the good. Playing endless games during endless summer days, on never-ending highways and in countless small towns...the wrong, the bad. Should he, or shouldn't he, the constantly bewildering question he'd begun asking himself.

"I was a homeboy, really, had a family and missed them. I loved baseball, always have and always will, but I just knew in my heart we were never going to get the chance to play in the majors...so I went home."

A man at the top of his game, playing not only with and against some of the best black baseball players, but arguably some of the greatest players...period! An educated man, who had seen humanity up close, not only as a ballplayer, but as a black man growing up in the South, then touring the North and Midwest. He lived with discrimination, felt the prejudice - why in the world would this change? It wouldn't and he knew it. Walking away from baseball was like walking away from a lover. Someone he'd given his heart and soul to, only to be told, you can't go there, you're, well...not good enough, talent being veiled as an excuse for intolerance and fear. The lover would leave a hole in his heart filled with regret and longing.

Home, of course, was Little Rock. Back to Christine, back to Dunbar High, back to his roots. He'd taught at Dunbar during the off season every year he'd played pro ball. The Negro League teams started practicing in May, but Byron wouldn't show up until school was out in late May. Now, for the first time in what seemed like a lifetime unto itself, he was going to be home year round. There was a certain serenity that came with his decision, not the least of which was being with Christine, but Little Rock and its ever-enduring milieu never changed.

"It was home, but it was still the same. At Dunbar we still got the hand-me-down books and even though we had the same education as the white teachers, we didn't make near as much as they did. But it was okay, I was home teaching, around my family, and not risking my life on the road."

The year was 1941, and for the next two years Byron would teach, coach some football, and spend time with Christine. This pseudo tranquility would end soon enough. The world was seemingly splitting at the seams, but due to continuing isolationist and neutralist pressure against entering the war, President Roosevelt made no formal declaration of war.

December 7, 1941, a day of infamy. Japan attacked Pearl Harbor and the United States declared war on the Empire of Japan, then one week later declared war on Germany and Italy.

As the country mustered its resources, Byron set his sights on what he could do to contribute. As had always been the norm in the South, he would be once again singled out as...inferior.

"I'd always wanted to go to medical school, but we just didn't have the money. So when it was time to enter the military, I tried to get in the medical corps. The color line was there, and it was rough. They told me they wouldn't take in colored, only whites. I told them, 'You'll have to draft me then,' and they did about three weeks later."

Thus began what Byron would call, "the worst three years of my life."

The war effort in America was unprecedented. Men and women of all backgrounds came together as never before. With the war increasing on two fronts in the South Pacific and in Europe, unity of endeavor was at an all-time high. Obligation and commitment, however, do not alter moral precepts. Almost 400,000 Latino Americans would serve on active duty during World War II, and proportionately receive more honors and decorations than any other ethnic group, but in 1943 the press castigated the "Zoot Suiters" (Mexican youth dressed in a distinctive style suit, called Zoot Suits) in southern California as foreigners, causing the "Zoot Suit Riots." Bands of soldiers and Marines stalked through the barrios, found Mexican and Latino youths dressed in their Zoot Suits, tore off their clothes, and beat them. The African Americans, however, were merely second-class citizens and treated accordingly. No one gave it another thought...except the black soldier.

"The black soldiers were treated badly. The only thing that saved me was some good advice from my dad. He said, 'Byron, you're not going to like this, the way they are going to treat you. But remember, don't do anything that will cause you to get a dishonorable discharge, because if you do, it will follow you the rest of your life.' I never forgot that."

The night before he left for the service, Byron stayed with his father and stepmother. He'd talked it over with Christine, and they both agreed it was the right thing to do. "I thought my mom was being pretty magnanimous," Jackie Benton, Byron's daughter said. "I mean, here it is the last night before he goes off to war, my mom not knowing if she'd ever see him again, and he goes over and spends the night with Papa Joe."

The next morning, as Byron stood at the door having said goodbye to his father, Papa Joe turned and called upstairs to Stella to come down and say goodbye. She refused. Stella had arrived on the heels of his mother's death, and Byron being the youngest, she sort of felt as if she'd raised him, and to a great extent she had. He was eleven years old when she married Papa Joe, and at the time she was only eleven years older than Byron. She'd opposed his marrying Christine, for the mere fact that Christine was taking him away. She and Christine would never get along. No matter what the family thought of Stella, she was devoted to and loved Joe. She was married to him for thirty years and cared for him the last nine of those following his stroke. When he died in 1952, she was heartbroken. After his burial she wanted to return to the cemetery, but the family felt it better if she didn't for a while. Driven by grief, she found a friend to take her and while grieving at the gravesite suffered a debilitating stroke. For the next six years, Byron would care for her.

She died alone in a nursing home, two years after Byron and his family moved to Denver.

But Byron would never forget her rejection that day. As deep as he felt the hurt, the effect on his father was even more profound. "I couldn't believe she wouldn't come down," he declared. "That's the only time I ever saw Papa cry."

Papa Joe was a sturdy man, not given to sentimentality or emotion. But life had worn on him. He'd lost his wife, one of his children, and now his youngest was going off to war, the war to end all wars. He would suffer a stroke while Byron was overseas.

"Papa was so strong. I'd never seen him sick, except that once in 1941. He got double pneumonia. The doctor told me he was very sick and to watch him. I sat right by his bed and watched him. About 3 a.m. he started to toss and turn, I grabbed him by his shoulders. He sat up and pushed me away. Suddenly, blood streamed out of his mouth all over me. I ran to the phone and called Dr. Ish. He showed up in his pajamas. I was sure Papa was going to die. Dr. Ish told me he was going to be fine. When he'd pushed me away he'd broken blood vessels in his lungs and cleaned out all that junk so he could breathe. It had saved his life. In about three days, he was out of bed and okay."

The stroke would not be so kind. One year after Byron reached Europe, he got word his father was ill. He found out it was a stroke and petitioned to come home, but they wouldn't let him. "I knew they'd let some white soldiers go home when this happened, but they told me I couldn't leave. I didn't get to see him till I was out of the service in 1945."

Papa Joe died in 1952, nine years after suffering a stroke that paralyzed the left side of his body. "Christine wrote me while I was in France and told me that he'd wait for me to get home...and he did."

It all started on maneuvers at Camp Claiborne in Louisiana. Byron served in the Quartermaster Corps. He was 32 years old and placed in an all-black regiment. Most of his comrades were in their early twenties and ill-equipped for what lay ahead. "All these boys were from Georgia and Tennessee, and lots of them couldn't read or write. I wound up teaching them."

"We always had to march in the back of the PX to get our meals. So one day, in France, they marched about fifty German prisoners right in the front door and let them sit down and eat right up front. Here we were getting ready to fight for our country and we had to come in the back and eat in the back. The enemy was getting treated better than us.... I had tried to get into the Officers Candidate School (OCS), but they told me we made better non-commissioned officers, but poor commissioned."

Their first stop overseas was in England. He was assigned to the Quartermaster Corps and spent nine months in Sherwood Forest training, living in the field, and preparing for D-Day.

Byron's unit landed at Normandy on June 11, 1944, five days after the initial assault and was in combat for the next 18 days.

"The night before our first fight, they came around and handed out grenades to all the men. We'd never been trained on how they worked or how to use them. I told the lieutenant I didn't think it was a very good idea. They finally decided we might be more dangerous to ourselves than the Germans and took them back. Our job was supply."

Due to the fact the military didn't think blacks made good commissioned officers, white officers were put in charge of black regiments. So was the case with Byron's regiment. "Our company commander was Captain Allen. He didn't like black soldiers and treated us that way. I didn't trust him 'cause he'd do whatever he had to, just to get ahead."

This was a low-grade assignment for white officers, and they only put up with it because they had to.

Allen was no different. Given his lot in the military, he decided to use his men in any way to gain favor with his superiors. Because Byron was older and respected by the men, Allen approached him with a proposal. "He asked me to be his snitch. Let him know what was going on with the men and what they thought of him. If I did this, he'd make me a first sergeant. I told him no!"

Allen found his man, however, in private first class Enoch Reed. "Reed would run and tell him every-thing...he made first sergeant," Byron remarked. "I never liked the man, but I guess that's what he thought he needed to do."

There were, however, men Byron liked, worked with, and lost. "Old Private Gooch, I really liked that man, but he was kinda crazy though. If they didn't watch him and he found some German prisoners alone, he'd shoot them. One day while we were in Paris, they called me to go get Gooch. He'd gone kind a nuts. I went and got him and everything was fine. We always got along."

Then there was John Mason, a proud man, dressed to the nines. He would spend the entire war with Byron. Huey Dotson, keeper of records, handled the mail and most importantly kept Byron informed about what Allen was up to. Octave Bradley, smart, educated, a liaison with headquarters. Sgt. Wood, who'd make sure Byron had steak and ham to eat. Sgt. Hines, the platoon sergeant, who treated the men well and earned their respect. Ralph Houston, a little man who loved to aggravate Allen, and loved to say to Byron, "I'm Ralph Houston, and I'm a son of a bitch." And, Herman Cowens, Byron's supply sergeant. "That man would work his tail off for me. Because he kept everything so neat and spotless, I won a few awards. One night he stayed up half the night arranging and cleaning weapons. Next morning the brass walked in and gave me an award. It was really him. I loved that man."

But then there was Clarence Davis. "I had to put Clarence on guard duty, and I hadn't been gone thirty minutes when someone called and told me he'd been killed. I wrote a letter to his mother and did all the paper work to get his body back home. I never heard from his people."

Toward the end of the war, Captain Allen called Byron into his office. "You've been worrying me about not getting into OCS," he told Byron. "Well, I've got something for you. If you'll stay around and work detonating mines, I'll make sure you get promoted and can go home an officer."

"I just stood there and looked at him," Byron remembered shaking his head. "Finally, I said, 'Can I ask you a question?' He nodded, so I asked, 'Are you gonna do it?' He didn't say anything, so I said, well, I'm scared too - I don't know nothin' about mines. I turned and walked out, that was the last time I ever saw him."

The segregated military lived on, even though the War Department abolished it on army posts. At the Battle of the Bulge in December, for the first time in United States military history black and white soldiers fought side by side when 2,500 African Americans volunteered to fight the Germans. When the battle ended, the troops went back to their segregated units.

On May 8, 1945, Germany surrendered, and President Truman declared V-E Day. On August 14, Japan surrendered following the bombing of Hiroshima and Nagasaki with atomic bombs. September 2 became known as V-J Day.

On December 26, 1945, Byron Johnson was honorably discharged from the U.S. Army. He headed home to his waiting wife, stricken father, and a country on the precipice of racial calamity.

12

During Byron's last year in the military, Jackie Robinson played his only season in Negro League ball. He was, ironically enough, the shortstop for the Kansas City Monarchs, Byron's old team and Byron's old position.

During the war, Byron hadn't thought much about baseball. Family, home, and survival were the concerns of the day. Baseball is of little importance when men are dying and you find yourself in a foreign country just trying to make another sunrise.

Meanwhile, back in America, Branch Rickey made a bold move and signed one Jack Roosevelt Robinson to a contract with the Brooklyn Dodgers minor league team playing in Montreal. This would forever change our National Pastime as well as American history, and for all intents and purposes, put an end to the Negro Leagues.

"He wasn't the best ballplayer in the Negro Leagues," Byron commented. "But he was the best man for the job. He was college educated and probably the best equipped to handle what was coming."

What was coming for Jackie Robinson was an odyssey through baseball that would transcend the world of sport in America like no other, then or now.

For Byron his return to Little Rock was all too familiar. The more things changed (WWII), the more they stayed the same (segregated South). The war had taken a toll on Byron, as it did with all who participated. He was suffering from a disease that affected the circulation in his hands, causing numbness and pain. He would find out, after the fact, that it was this condition that led to his hypertension. This malady would eventually lead to his having to quit teaching and coaching.

"I think trying to work with the kids and all the problems surrounding education in Little Rock after the war just piled up on him," his daughter Jackie said. "The doctor finally told him he had to quit, it was killing him. He was nervous and couldn't sleep. That was rough for him because he loved teaching. He never told me he missed it...but, I know he did."

When the school year ended in 1946, Byron retired from teaching. The only decent job for a black man, other than teaching, was with the U.S. Postal Service. That summer he went to work for them as a carrier; black men weren't allowed to be clerks early on, no matter what their education and background. It was certainly different from teaching, but there was actually a part of the job that was cathartic. He was outdoors, walking, and the hypertension began to subside. Later that year he would, amazingly enough, be promoted to clerk, and a clerk he would stay till he and his family moved away over a decade later.

Life had settled back into an old proverbial pattern. Byron clerked at the local post office, and Christine taught school at Stephens Elementary, where they had both gone to school as kids. Little changed in Little Rock, while on the American landscape, change on the racial front was in its embryonic stage in the truest sense of equality.

In 1947, President Truman created the Presidential Committee on Civil Rights to study existing federal civil rights protections and ways to improve them. In Virginia, Irene Morgan, an African American, refused to move from the front of a Greyhound Bus to the back. She won a ruling, *Morgan vs Commonwealth of Virginia,* that invalidated segregation on interstate buses, setting a precedent for future challenges of segregation in public facilities.

As their lives floated along, Byron and Christine settled into a sort of false contentment. As kids growing up in Little Rock, they were a little more impervious to the racial slurs and indignities, but now as adults, not only having to put up with it themselves, they saw it on the faces of the children, and it penetrated and stung.

"When I was about 8 or 9 and we'd walk to school, we had to go by this house owned by Mrs. Durwood," Byron recalled in disbelief. "She had this big green parrot she'd put out on the front porch. As we'd walk by it would say, 'Here come the niggers.' Back then we'd just try to ignore it, but later when I thought about it...well, what can you say?"

With all the palpable racial discord, it was still home. They were Southerners, as had been their parents and their grandparents. There was a certain comfort with that. Despite all the uncertainty, they had each other, and now were presented with some new and exciting news. Christine was pregnant. What had been home for just the two of them was now going to be home for their first child. Beyond the exhilaration was a responsibility neither had ever faced before. The roots sank more deeply with a determination to make this not only a home, but a harbor of safety and love. A place where their child could grow up with more opportunity to flourish and develop into a citizen of

America, not just the South, replete with all the rights and privileges promised by the founding fathers.

Idealism, however, is a capricious notion when cast against the tide of bigotry. With all good intentions and resolve, the ever-present and ugly face of discrimination would manifest itself once again. This time with Little Rock being the epicenter of hate and conflict, and Byron would find himself right in the middle of it.

13

As the clouds of abhorrence began to billow in the South, Byron and Christine found a silver lining. Jacquelyn Elizabeth Johnson came into the world on July 26, 1947. A beautiful baby girl to be raised in the same city and neighborhood her parents had been reared in. The city had changed little, but the circumstances under which she would grow up would be more dramatic and heated than those of her parents.

"When you're real little you don't know you're being discriminated against," Jackie said. "But once you get to school and realize you're getting hand-me-downs and leftovers...then you know. You see it and feel it."

She attended Stephens Elementary School, where her parents had gone and where her mother was still teaching. A few blocks away her cousin, Carlotta

Walls, who was five years older, would within a few years embark on a life-altering journey. Not only her life, but also the lives of Byron, Christine, Jacquelyn and every black student in America.

"The first time I ever remember seeing Byron was the day Jackie was born," Carlotta noted. "I must have been about four, and he was supervising the playground at Stephens. My mother had dropped me off so she could go to the hospital for Jackie's birth. There were these boys with slingshots, shooting rocks. I wanted to shoot one so bad and I kept asking them if they'd let me. Finally, one of them said okay and handed me the slingshot. I picked up a rock, pulled the sling back and shot myself right in the mouth. I was holding it the wrong way. It knocked out some of my teeth and I was lying there bleeding all over the place. The first face I saw was Byron's. He was standing over me telling me I'd be okay. He picked me up, and they took me to the doctor. I was okay, but I'll never forget how caring he was."

Byron's compassion and strength would come into play a few years later when Carlotta was older and in greater need of it. They would form a bond that would last the rest of their lives.

The year was 1954, the culmination of events leading up to *Brown vs Board of Education of Topeka*. Jackie was six and Carlotta was eleven. And Byron and

Christine were blessed with another child. Joseph Byron Johnson would make his appearance on February 5. He was cute and definitely had an outgoing personality right from the beginning.

The Supreme Court had unanimously declared that separating public school students by race violated black children's constitutional rights. There had been several episodes in this chapter of American history, starting in 1896 with *Plessy vs Ferguson* where the Supreme Court upheld Louisiana law requiring railroads to provide "equal but separate accommodations for the white and colored races." This ruling had become the legal underpinning for widespread racial segregation in public schools. Then in 1899 the first school segregation case reached the Supreme Court. The justices abided unequal treatment, refusing to force Augusta, Georgia to close a high school for whites until it reopened a black school.

By 1954, segregation, integration, separate but equal, had all come to a boil. No longer a smoldering concept, or a distant drum. Confrontation was just a matter of time. With the *Brown* ruling many thought relief was on the way, justice would be served. But in the South, time and custom is deliberate, measured and unyielding.

"Most folks felt the battle had been won," commented

Brumit DeLaine, a retired school administrator and teacher whose father, Reverend J.A. DeLaine, was the organizing genius behind a Clarendon, South Carolina, protest that led to *Briggs vs Elliott*, one of five school equality cases the Supreme Court consolidated into *Brown vs School Board*. Reverend DeLaine had initiated parent petitions calling for equal access to public school transportation for black students. But legal rulings do not change minds or alter the teachings of racism. "Everybody who signed those petitions, plain old common people, suffered consequences," said Brumit DeLaine, who was an eleventh grader in 1954. Landowners evicted sharecroppers who had worked their properties for decades. White employers fired black employees, including Reverend DeLaine and three other teachers in his family. Businesses serving black customers were pushed into ruin, and Reverend DeLaine was run out of town and his home burned to the ground. Having found a new hometown, he saw his church destroyed and his home attacked in a nighttime shooting.

The *Brown vs Board of Education* ruling was merely the tip of the iceberg. What would follow in 1957 was the true beginning of change in public education. It would be frightening and shocking and most importantly public. The nation would at last see, via television, what had been going on in the South for years, and Central High School in Little Rock, Arkansas would be the focal point.

The pain Carlotta had suffered on the playground would now pale in comparison to what she was about to undergo. This would not be self- inflicted as then, this would come from hate fermenting over decades, odium that would boil over on nine black students trying to attend a white high school. The President, the Arkansas Governor, the courts and the nation would watch as these nine young black students challenged the very soul of bigotry. Carlotta Walls was one of these nine.

Born to Cartelyou and Juanita Walls, Carlotta was one of three daughters, she being the oldest. Her two younger sisters, Loujuana, 11 and Tina, 5, had anything but ordinary lives themselves. "My sisters' upbringing was not normal. The spotlight was always on me."

"I was taught to accept challenges, not to turn away," Carlotta stated. "Making C's was not acceptable, only A's and B's. It's one of the reasons I persevered. It actually became like a job to me, that's how I looked at it, but success was required by my parents."

And successful she was. She would make the honor roll and National Honor Society and be one of only two of the original nine to graduate from Central High School in 1960.

"The first day of school was always a good day," she remembered. "I had never missed a day of school since I started in the first grade." But none of her previous first days at school would come close to this. Not in magnitude or significance, not only for her but the nation.

September 4, 1957: this was to be the official first day for these nine black students entering all-white Central High School. It was not to be. Governor Orval Faubus had called in the National Guard to deny them entry. This, coupled with the riotous crowd, forced a delay in starting. "We did not expect this," said Juanita Walls, Carlotta's mother. "We were in shock, and, yes, I did worry about her safety, but it was my faith in God that carried me through."

The "Little Rock Nine," as they would come to be known, met at 13th and Park Streets that first day, only they were eight. Elizabeth Eckford hadn't gotten the message and was forced to meet the rebellion outside the school alone. Amid threats of unspeakable violence and lynching, she tried to duck into a drugstore. Unsuccessful she now turned and faced the vicious crowd. "I tried to see a friendly face somewhere in the mob – someone who maybe would help," she said. "I looked into the face of an old woman, and it seemed a kind face, but when I looked at her again, she spat on me."

They would not get to return to school until September 23, and only then after a federal judge denied a school board request to suspend the integration plan. In full view of a nation in shock, rioting once again broke out and the Nine had to be smuggled out a side door before noon. This would be an omen of what the rest of the year would hold for the Little Rock Nine.

President Dwight Eisenhower, calling the rioting "disgraceful," called in the 101st Airborne Division, who only years before had been the first paratroopers ever used in warfare. Now, sadly, here they were at home defending American from fellow American. On Sept. 25, the third attempt at a full day of school, they were escorted into the building by the soldiers, and each child was assigned a bodyguard.

"We were told if we retaliated in any way we would be expelled," Carlotta remembered. "I had never been taught to fight or hate, but there was this redheaded girl who loved to walk on the back of my feet. Since I had to avoid confrontation I chose to just walk faster, so she couldn't keep up with me. We were supposed to have our guards for two weeks, but I noticed I was getting a new guard every week. I could really move when I had to, and I guess I was just wearing the guards out, so they changed every week."

Once the 101st Airborne left and the Arkansas National Guard took over, things deteriorated quickly. Harassment and intimidation took over inside Central High. The National Guard was more indifferent, with many of them feeling this was wrong, that it was being forced on them. Gloria Ray was hit with a rock and pushed down a flight of stairs. Minnijean Brown was expelled for dumping her lunchroom chili on antagonists, and two white students were suspended for wearing signs that read, "One down...eight to go." With bleeding heels and badly bruised legs, Carlotta persevered, making the honor roll.

Byron's role, although not in the forefront, was nonetheless important, especially to Carlotta. Since the start of their education had been delayed for three weeks, they were behind academically. "We had a lot of catching up to do...we had to be "Super Negroes," Carlotta said emphatically. "We had tutors, both black and white, from a local college the last two weeks. They helped us get caught up. Uncle Byron helped me with my biology homework, because that's what he taught. He was a big help."

He also helped in transport. Since her father had been ostracized and was now forced to find work outside the city as a bricklayer, getting Carlotta to and from Central High School fell to others, such as Byron and Daisy Bates, a black woman who risked her life on numerous occasions to see that Carlotta and the others made it safely to school. "He would put me in the back seat of the car and then we'd go pick up Carlotta," Byron's daughter Jackie remembered. "We'd have to drive through rioters. They'd stand in the way and then start rocking the car back and forth. It was terrifying."

Terrifying was an understatement of what happened to those nine black students that year. There were basically three groups in the school. First, foremost and most obvious, were the troublemakers, the ones given to hate and intimidation. The second was the "I wish this would just go away" group, of which Carlotta was one. Third, and most admirable, were the white students who actually tried to help. As would be expected under those conditions, they were persecuted and ostracized for their efforts and caring.

Not only was the school seething with acrimony, but the entire community was in turmoil. Rioters surrounded the school, malcontents milled through town, and blacks throughout the city feared for their lives. One such incident occurred just down the street from the Johnson household. While the father sat on the front porch protecting his property, white insurgents sneaked in the back door, dragged his young son out and beat him to death in the backyard. Byron began carrying a gun in the car. The police, sensing this might be the case with the black citizenry, began stopping black drivers and arresting them, if they found weapons. Byron removed the gun and kept it at home on a table by the front door.

As tensions grew during the year, Sheriff Dean Smith stepped forward out of duty, and not moral conviction, to quell rioters intent on breaking into the school. He'd even been forced to have his men fire off some warning shots to disperse the angry mob. He was a man alone. Even though he didn't truly believe in what he was doing, he was a man of responsibility and tried to live up to the letter of the law. Ultimately, it became a high price to pay. For his efforts he was persecuted and, ironically enough, discriminated against. At odds with not only the community, but his own wife, he took his own life as well as his wife's a few years later.

Governor Faubus closed all four Little Rock high schools for the 1958-59 school year pending a public vote on integration. Eight of the Little Rock Nine went out of state to study, with only Carlotta staying and taking correspondence courses through the University of Arkansas. She and Jefferson Thomas were the only two to return to Central High School for their senior year. "After that first year, I didn't have to go back," she said. "But I had to validate that first year with my diploma."

February 9, 1960, during Carlotta's senior year, was a day she and her family would never forget. The entire school year had been punctuated with action and reaction, attack and retaliation. But this rainy night in Little Rock would live forever in the annals of disgust and racism. Carlotta's father was working that night at his father's restaurant. Carlotta, her mother, and two sisters were at home talking in one of the back bedrooms. What sounded to neighbors like a gigantic clap of thunder, was in fact the front of the Walls house being blown off by a bomb. Fortunately, none of them were injured, but the front of the house was destroyed. In what can only be described as a complete miscarriage of justice, the FBI arrested Mr. Walls for blowing up his own house. "My father was held by the FBI for 72 hours for bombing his own home," Carlotta stated in complete disbelief. "I'd never seen him cry or even get tears in his eyes. He did that day. He was walking down the hill toward home from the bus after he was released, and he was crying. I'll never forget that image." To this day she cannot discuss it without tearing up.

Cartelyou Walls had fought in World War II to free the oppressed in Europe. Now, in his own hometown, he was being singled out simply because he was black. His life was never the same after that. He died of leukemia at the age of 53 in 1976. He is buried in Fort Logan National Cemetery, along with other defenders of freedom, in Denver, Colorado.

The FBI then arrested Herbert Monts, a neighbor and friend of Carlotta's, for the bombing. He was sent to prison for five years for a crime he didn't commit. Years later the Klu Klux Klan admitted they were behind the bombing.

Carlotta, would go on to Michigan State University, and meet the likes of Thelonius Monk and Malcolm X and become friends with President Bill Clinton. She and her family moved to Denver in 1963, mostly at the urging of Byron. He'd moved his family to the Mile High City in 1958 and told Carlotta it was a great place to bring up a family. She still resides there, selling real estate and traveling the country, telling the never-to-be-forgotten story of the Little Rock Nine.

"You know my grandfather was a very outspoken man and didn't think of himself as black or white...just a man. He used to go hunting with Papa Joe, Byron's father. Sometimes his outspokenness was a problem for blacks and whites, but he meant well. One of the amazing ironies of this story is that in 1927 when Central High School was built, my grandfather was one of the brick-masons."

Congress passed the Civil Rights Act of 1957, the first Civil Rights bill since Reconstruction, to safeguard any U.S. citizen's voting rights by setting penalties for violations of this privilege. This also created the Civil

Rights Commission to advise Congress on creating Civil Rights policy and law. The legislation was vigorously opposed, especially by South Carolina Senator Strom Thurmond, who set a record for the longest filibuster, speaking nonstop for twenty-four hours and twenty-seven minutes.

In the Major Leagues, black ballplayers were now proven stars. Men who'd started their careers in the old Negro Leagues. Players like Willie Mays, who'd gotten his start in baseball playing for the Birmingham Black Barons in 1948. He would go on to become what many consider the greatest player ever. Roy Campanella, who played for the Baltimore Elite Giants for nine years, became one of the most celebrated catchers in Dodger history, before his career was tragically cut short by a near fatal auto accident in 1958. And, of course, Henry Louis (Hank) Aaron, who also started his illustrious career playing shortstop with the Indianapolis Clowns in 1952. Twenty-three years and 755 home runs later, he ended his profession as the greatest homerun hitter of all time.

These were all men who only years earlier would not have been allowed on the same field with Major League players. Baseball had changed. The last National League team to break the color barrier, the Philadelphia Phillies, brought aboard black infielder, John Kennedy in 1957, while the last American League team was the Boston Red Sox, who in 1959 signed Elijah "Pumpsie" Green. America, too, was changing, but not as swiftly, and not without rancor. The South was still THE SOUTH and the Johnsons had had enough. In the Spring of 1958 they left...and never went back.

14

What a difference a thousand miles makes. Not just the distance from Little Rock to Denver, but the distance between outright bigotry and perceived acceptance.

"In the South you knew where you stood," Jackie recalled. "They didn't like you, you knew your place and that was it. But in Denver, it was more subtle. They'd say one thing to your face, and act differently behind your back."

It's a strange crossing moving from the South to the West. Leaving your roots and the culture you'd grown up in, albeit oppressive, behind, then heading west to a new life, in a new place with what appeared to be new values. There is always a gain and loss; the trick is to recognize one from the other. The gains surface quickly, are more obvious by comparison, but the losses, those can be more faint, taking a while to be truly understood.

"Denver was so different from Little Rock," Jackie remembered. "The weather, the schools and the way black people were treated...it was unbelievable."

A reverie they'd had for a year. Having visited in 1957, staying with Christine's brother, they'd returned to Little Rock and started planning their move. Returning in the late spring of 1958 they again moved in with Mike Torrence, Christine's brother, at 3410 E. 30th Avenue. This was just a few blocks from what was then called Sportland Park. Jackie was 10 and Joe was 4.

"They had a swimming pool at Sportland and I could walk over there and go swimming...actually go swimming with everybody else, black and white," Jackie said, smiling. "That was new for me, and I did it a lot."

This was but one of the new facets of their life in Denver. After staying with Uncle Mike, for several months they moved into an apartment on Elizabeth Street, two blocks from Columbine Elementary School. Christine got a job as a permanent supply teacher at Columbine while Byron worked nights at the Post Office next to Union Station in downtown Denver. This way he could take care of Joe during the day, and Christine was home at night. Jackie caught the bus by their apartment taking her to Smiley Junior High School, a school that would become a focal point of their lives a few years later.

Life was good. Within a few months they bought their first home at 2954 Clermont Street. "We bought that house on Clermont from the Wallaces," Byron remembered fondly. "We drew the contract up at night...I fell in love with that house. We'd go over at night and just look at it. We had to wait a month till they moved out. It had hot water heat, which was new to us. We had new carpet put in. We took Joe over, boy he looked good crawling around on that new carpet."

This was more than just a new house, it was a statement, a statement of value, of arrival. "My father felt like he'd made it. Bought a home for his family...it was really something," Jackie commented.

But with change, even positive change, comes concern. Jackie had never gone to school with white students and was now going to be in the minority for the first time in her life. Byron and Christine were apprehensive. "I'd never gone to a segregated school before and my parents were nervous about it," she recalled. "I had to take some tests, and we didn't know what the standards were here. I did fine, which told us something about the quality of education in Little Rock."

The educational gain was a new school, new books, classes not offered to her at old Gibbs Elementary in Little Rock, like music, gym and art. Gibbs was a sorry place as an educational edifice. The third floor had been condemned for fear the floor might collapse. The building had bats in it, and all the books they had to use were in as bad a shape as the school. But in the midst of this house of cards was a silver lining. All black students – all black teachers. "They cared about us, how we did," Jackie remembered. "We had to toe the mark, there was no social promotion. We had a sense of community, and they taught us about black history and literature. Don't get me wrong, I had wonderful teachers in Denver, but you'd have never known there was any black history or that a black person had ever written a book."

Beyond the obvious changes, the more delicate change of attitude was taking place. Growing up in a virtually all-black community, your mindset is of that culture. Moving into a mixed community brings about a more pronounced, what W. E. B. Du Bois called "double-consciousness." In his *The Souls of Black Folk,* published in 1903, he talked about this process called "otherness." Being black in a white culture evokes a way of acting, writing, and talking that is not true to one's heritage. It isn't necessarily a choice as much as a tactic of survival. Maya Angelou discusses this in her autobiography, *I Know Why The Caged Bird Sings.* Sadly this book has been banned in some schools and libraries. When talking to whites, Maya might phrase something appropriately for that situation, but back in her neighborhood with her friends she'd say it like she meant it.

This conditioned reflex would soon be a part of Byron's work environment. Other than his military experience, he'd never been placed in such a WHITE circumstance. The general feeling at the post office was if you were black and from the South...well, you couldn't be too smart. This, of course, belied the fact that Byron had a college education, had been a teacher and loved to quote from Shakespeare, Edgar Allan Poe, and Langston Hughes. Nevertheless, his boss seemed irritated by the fact that Byron might want to advance. He put him in a position to train new recruits, then proceeded to promote them above Byron once they were through training. As a man never given to using his skin color as leverage, Byron felt betrayed and discriminated against. Here they were starting a new life in Denver, and those old feelings and old hurts were resurfacing. It appeared his boss was going out of his way to keep him down. After discussing it with Christine, he obtained a lawyer and brought a discrimination suit against the post office. He was the first black man to do so in the state of Colorado.

Byron would eventually lose the case, but he felt it was necessary, required, sometimes you just have to make a stand. In the South, you might have been hung for attempting something so...radical. But in Denver you just lost the case and moved on. Work at the post office had become intolerable while the suit was going on. Byron's supervisor had become even more adamant about making him pay for his insubordination.

Byron had gotten back into ball while at the post office, playing for their branch softball team. It was fun, certainly not baseball, but fun. And for the first time his entire family could see him play. He was nearing fifty so the quick reflexes and speed were not what they used to be, but he could still hit and still throw.

Life was back on track. Jackie and Joe were in school doing well, and Christine was teaching. Circumstances at the post office weren't good, but with everything else in his life going well, he could put up with the situation at the post office.

In 1962, Carlotta came to live with the Johnsons. She lived with them for one year, before her family moved to Denver. As the Johnsons rolled into the 1960s, all was well, or at least they thought so. The latter part of the decade, however, would be one of the saddest and most painful in their lives.

15

The 1960s would not only be a tumultuous decade for the Johnsons but for America as well. Coming out of the late 1950s, the first, albeit small, steps were taken into integration, whereas the 1960s would become strides of decisiveness.

For blacks in the 1950s, things had become hip and cool, and for the most part, white culture was corny. As they grew into the 1960s, their perceptions changed. Just being cool, and viewing the establishment as banal was not enough. Action needed to be taken, voices heard, changes needed to be made, and through unification and the establishment of their own leaders the movement was formed.

Men like Malcolm X, Martin Luther King, Jr., and Langston Hughes, and women like Rosa Parks, Ella Baker, and Fannie Lou Hamer, stepped forward. They were individuals of passion and determination, who although controversial in their own way, established and gave life to the black movement. The Society of Umbra, a collection of young African American writers, artists, and musicians was formed and gave the cause visibility and a voice.

In February of 1960, African American college students conducted a sit-in at F.W. Woolworth's in Greensboro, North Carolina at the lunch counter after four black students had been denied service. This would be the start of many such sit-ins, mostly in the South, and the movement carried over from restaurants to libraries to movie theaters. In 1961 President John F. Kennedy took office, quickly forming the Peace Corps and the Committee on Equal Employment Opportunity, spawning the term "affirmative action."

Things were moving forward in the black community, not as fast as some would like, but with a new hope. As Ishmael Reed said when he heard President Kennedy on television ordering the University of Mississippi to integrate, "We'd never heard a president talk like that." There would be more rhetoric on both sides, some positive, some negative, but always thought-provoking. And as is always the case with change: resistance, anger and violence would follow.

In June of 1963, Medgar Evers was shot to death

while getting out of his car in Jackson, Mississippi, making him a hero and martyr of the Civil Rights movement. In August, 250,000 people marched on Washington D.C., where Martin Luther King, Jr., delivered his famous "I Have a Dream" speech. Eighteen days later in Birmingham, Alabama, which had become known as "Johannesburg of America" for its fervent and sometimes violent refusal to comply with Civil Rights laws, four African American girls were killed by a bomb explosion while attending Sunday school at the Sixteenth Street Baptist Church. In November of that same year President John F. Kennedy was assassinated in Dallas, Texas. With the country trying to climb out of its mourning stupor and the confrontation beginning to heat up in Viet Nam, civil rights had suddenly eased to the back of the bus.

The Johnsons were moving forward, but keeping a watchful eye on the national events. Denver to a great extent was untouched, at least as far as a big municipality could be, by the racial hatred, but prejudice, although somewhat veiled, was still evident. The city had its "cultural communities" and even though assimilation was accepted throughout the city, invisible boundaries did exist.

In the early to mid-1960s there were approximately 30,000 blacks living in the Denver area and only about 60,000 in the entire State of Colorado. Of the 30,000, virtually none of them lived south of Colfax Avenue. They resided on the northeast side of the city. The Johnsons were one of these families. As Carlotta stated, however, "In Denver you hoped to be treated like a person, as opposed to being treated like a black man or woman, and for the most part we were. But we knew there were areas we were probably better off not venturing into."

In 1966 Byron was still working nights at the post office, Christine was teaching at Stedman Elementary School, Jackie was in college at Colorado State College in Greeley, Colorado, and Joe was in his first year at Smiley Jr. High School. The assassination of President Kennedy, although still palpable in the hearts of Americans, was being overshadowed by the "conflict" in southeast Asia. By September, the U.S. had a total of 300,000 troops in Viet Nam, where 5,008 would be killed by the year's end.

As the advancement of Civil Rights waned, the concept of "Black Power" began to form. The notion was debated by various African American organizations including the NAACP, who rejected it. In October, Huey Newton and Bobby Seale establish the Black Panther Party For Self Defense in Oakland, California. Their demands, some of which were outlandish (freedom for all black prisoners), along with a militant, revolutionist style, provoked persecution from local, state, and federal authorities.

As with most blacks at the time, Byron and Christine wanted a peaceful solution to racism. Their feeling was violence would only beget violence, and they'd seen and felt enough of that. Their daughter was attending an integrated college, and their son was excelling at an integrated junior high school. Byron was spending time coaching and working with youth groups, mostly through their church, Park Hill United Methodist. Their lives were productive and serene, exactly what they'd hoped for when they left Little Rock.

Across America, however, this would be known as the "hot summer" due to the worst urban riots in U.S. history, but not in Denver. "We fell in love with Denver the first time we came here," Byron recalled. "And that never changed." What was about to change though was the Johnson family.

Joseph Byron Johnson, named after his father and grandfather, was not only an outstanding student, but a gifted athlete. He excelled in football and baseball (curious) and became an outstanding basketball player as well. He was exceedingly popular, not only with his fellow students at Smiley Jr. High, but with the teachers and administrators as well.

"Joe won friends easily among boys, because he was an outstanding baseball, as well as football, player," according to Clyde Langley, who had Joe in physical education from first through sixth grades at Stedman Elementary School. "He was a tremendous leader of the other kids as well as a great athlete."

"He had a real concern for all his classmates," said Jim Daniels of the Denver Public Schools Community Relations Office, who taught Joe at Stedman (and was the only black teacher Joe ever had).

"I never saw a child who was always in such a happy mood," said Miss Susan Roos, a Smiley art teacher. "Yet he wasn't 'overly nice.'"

"One thing was always his willingness to work – to help the other students, to help the teachers and to listen, too. This stood out," said Tony De Camillis, Smiley counselor and social studies teacher. "He got his work done, but he wasn't square."

He definitely wasn't square. In fact he was considered one of the coolest kids in school. This, of course, was a sentiment exuded by his peers. Joe was not only helpful to the instructors, but was ready to assist his fellow students at the drop of a hat. "In elementary school, he'd always take up for the girls," Belinda Knight said.

"Another thing – he could give a person good advice. We'd try to do what he'd say, and no matter what the problem was, it would usually work out," remembered Aundra Lewis. But he was a kid who would only give advice if you asked for it."

"We became real good friends, though we never spent too much time together," Sue Winter said. "The day after Martin Luther King was shot we were having trouble, and a boy I knew was beat up by a gang. Joe explained the black power movement to me. He really didn't seem to take a side. He was just trying to explain to me how some of these kids felt; how maybe they were underprivileged."

Joe was special, not only in the classroom, but on the athletic field. Not only away from school, but in his own home. "Joe was one of the finest kids I've every known, but I think he was just an extension of his parents," said Joe Harvat of the school's Community Relations Office."

"You can't say enough good about Joe and his parents," agreed Bill Lee, a coach at Smiley. "The Johnsons rounded up – or purchased – a lot of equipment for the Falcons (Joe's Young American League football team). They made it possible for a lot of kids to play who wouldn't have played otherwise."

"I respected Joe's folks a whole lot," said Pete Wehner an East High School student. "They did a lot for integration and Joe had real good moral standards."

"He loved sports," Byron recalled. "He played football and baseball, and I taught him how to play. He played third base. He was good in football, but better in baseball."

With Jackie up in Greeley in school, Byron began to focus on Joe's athletic career. "They were inseparable, hooked at the hip," remembered Carlotta. "Wherever Byron was, so was Joe, and vise versa."

"I think we were uniquely close," said Joe's mom. "Whenever his sister Jackie was in an activity, well, we'd all go to that. If it was Joe's game, we'd all be there. Joe was very proud of his family. He was awfully proud I was a teacher; he was proud of his father, he was proud of his sister, and he was proud of his friends and wanted us to meet them."

Joe used to go along to the Dahlia Lanes when his father took Jackie and her friends from Denver East High School there for bowling meets. He attracted the attention of Sonny Liston, former heavyweight boxing champion, who made his home in Denver.

"Joe had what we call very good form," his father said. "Sonny noticed him and started talking to him."

Before long, Sonny introduced Joe to his friends, former Denver Bronco football players, Cookie Gilchrist and Odell Barry. The trio attended football banquets and school assemblies for Joe. Sonny and Joe played golf together. Gilchrist gave Joe his 10-speed bike and Joe rode it for miles, even into the mountains. When Liston moved to Las Vegas, Nevada, he gave Joe his desk and 10-volume encyclopedia of science. At Christmas he sent him a radio.

"I don't know why Sonny did so much for Joe," Mrs. Johnson said wonderingly.

"Sonny said if he had a son he would want him to be like Joe," Byron said.

In the Spring of 1967 Byron and Joe were at a golf exhibition between Arnold Palmer and Art Wall at the Denver Country Club. "Joe complained about his knee aching and that he didn't feel good," Byron remembered.

Carlotta happened to be at the same exhibition. "I ran into them and Byron had Joe's wrists under some cold running water to cool him down. He didn't look good."

Not only did he not look good...he wasn't good. Joe was sick, and that summer was diagnosed with lupus erythematous. This is usually a disease that strikes adult women. It's a steady and progressive deterioration of the whole body.

Margaret Burney, the school nurse at Smiley, learned of the diagnosis soon after it was made. For more than a year, however, she kept up the pretense among students that Joe suffered from "a kidney disease." "I didn't want them to know the prognosis; I didn't want Joe to know."

Slowly but surely the insidious illness began to take its toll. As his body became more frail and tender, Joe was forced to give things up. First were his sports, baseball, football, and basketball. He loved them so much, but his body just wouldn't let him participate any more. He took up golf and pool, with Byron even putting a pool table in their basement. And, as was always the case, he became highly skilled in both.

"He had a pool table in his basement," said Gordon Pryor, a fellow student. "I got kinda tired of playing him; I think I beat him twice."

In golf he stood out as well. He tied for second in a junior putting tourney sponsored by the East Denver Golf Club. When he could no longer take part in physical activities, he turned his attention to student government.

In the spring of 1967, Joe's friend, Sue Winter, asked him to run for Head Boy. He won easily, but once school ended and summer heated up, Joe was hospitalized for the first time. During that time the principal and staff were meeting with the PTA, trying to get the viewpoint of the students. "Joe was ill," Principal Harold Scott said. "So he sent his mother to the meeting, and he had written a beautiful letter in which he suggested the motto for the year be 'SOS – Superior Outlook for Smiley.' He was very concerned about improving the image of Smiley and about more involvement for the boys and girls in the school."

Later that summer, however, Joe was able to attend the Leadership Camp for student council members in Colorado at Pinehurst Country Club. Sue remembered how, during square dancing, Joe was accidentally hit in the area of his kidney – now agonizingly tender – and he doubled over and cried. "He was really sick that night," she said. "But he was looking forward to the regular dance the next night. He could really dance and had a wonderful time."

When September rolled around and it was time for school, he was unable to present his speech as Head Boy. He was in the hospital again. He asked Sue, who had been elected Secretary of the Executive Council, to read his message. It was Sept. 17, Citizenship Day, and his message belied his age and experience.

It read: "Today our country is in deep trouble because there are many American citizens who are not enjoying those rights, privileges, and freedoms promised by our Constitution.

"Until the time we are old enough to vote, to right these wrongs, we can take advantage of the opportunities made available to us at Smiley to prepare for active participation in our country's government in the future."

He listed three qualities he felt were important for Smiley's students: "First; courtesy, kindness, friendliness, respect for each other and a willingness to work together for the good of Smiley.

"Second; Character – that something which will bring out in each of us confidence in our ability to assume responsibility, and to do our best, honestly and fairly."

"And most of all; Courage. To be able to 'keep your cool' when sometimes you feel like 'blowing your stack.' To hang in there and stick it out when the going gets tough, especially if we know that it's the best thing for something worthwhile."

"These are the qualities which will result in good citizenship in our school, our community and our country. These are the qualities that will help us to make this school year a Superior One for Smiley."

That same week, Joe, suffered numerous convulsions. The disease had gotten the upper hand on this small, but mighty young man. There were letters, many, many letters from school, from friends, and kids he'd never met. The outpouring was overwhelming. His mom would spend nights with him in the hospital and his dad during the day. His sister would come as often as possible, and Nurse Burney was there constantly.

By November, Joe's journey on earth was coming to an end. He was weak and frail, but still had a spirit that would light up a room. "Joey was just kind of a pet to all of us," said Mrs. Phyllis Schroeder, a nurse at Rose Memorial Hospital. "He was very patient with us. Very seldom did we hear him complain, and he had every reason in the world to complain. That family was just great, and Joe was great for them, he was just everything to them."

On November 24, Joe's breathing became irregular and labored. He appeared ready to go to sleep. He rolled over on his side, his breathing quieted and he passed away.

Reverend Gene McCornack, from Greeley, whose son had attended Stedman Elementary School with Joe wrote the following letter to Byron and Christine:

"I know that my son is a better boy for having had Joe as a friend and as you know that means a great deal to a parent.

"Thank you for helping Joe to become the fine person he was, and my faith in the wisdom of God is that he would not allow the joy and enthusiasm of a Joe Johnson to be wasted just because the body couldn't bear the burdens of life. I believe in God's promise of eternal life with a new 'spiritual body' fit for the new existence beyond our logical understanding..."

Joe had written in an autograph book he kept in his room at the hospital, "Happiness is being remembered, and finding out there were so many who cared when I was sick and in the hospital."

The last words he said to Byron were, "Dad, I've been to the mountain top, and I'm going to be okay."

16

The year 1968 would not only end sadly for the Johnson family, but for America and the Civil Rights movement as well. In April, Martin Luther King, Jr., was assassinated in Memphis, Tennessee, where he was providing support for striking sanitation workers. Riots ensued across the nation.

In June, Robert F. Kennedy was assassinated in Los Angeles, shortly after winning the California Democratic Party's presidential primary.

With every step forward, there always seemed to be two steps backward. So it was with Byron and Christine. It's not natural to have your children predecease you. Death is always expected, although not explicitly thought about or spoken of, but when you lose your child all that changes. The pain is deep, leaving a hole that will never be filled. A hole Byron feels to this day. With the painful 1960s behind them, Byron and Christine entered the decade of the 1970s with quasi hope. Their son was gone, but only in reality; he was still alive in their hearts and souls.

"It's kind of like starting over," Byron said. "You're angry and not sure what to do, all you know is, he's gone."

But start over you must, for life beckons. Losing one of your children is not for the faint of heart. It requires a strength and courage no one feels he or she can summon. So it was with Byron and Christine, but they were raised with a faith and determination that would now be tested, and as they always had, they overcame. Not the sense of loss, that would never go away, but the realization that life in fact continues on, and they had a wonderful daughter and now an even more special granddaughter. This then, would help them refocus, not on sorrow, but on the wonder of what they still had.

As Jackie's daughter Lisa turned three in 1970, Byron and Christine found themselves drawn to her as if she imparted some of Joe in her very being. "I always felt," Jackie, said, "Lisa carried some of Joe's spirit in her." Whether it was his spirit, no one knows, but as she grew there was an eminence that was unmistakable.

"You know, there's that old saying, 'When the sun goes down on one life, so it rises on another,' and looking back, I guess that's kind of how we felt," Jackie remembered. "Lisa was born in December of 1967 and Joe died in November of 1968. We have a picture of him holding her when she was a baby."

As the Johnson family changed their lives, tried to readjust, America seemed to waver in its evolution concerning civil rights. As Byron watched and noted how blacks had become almost icons on the baseball fields, in mainstream society, progress was less...forthcoming.

"I couldn't believe how some of these ballplayers were such heroes," Byron commented, "But away from the ball park, well, things were still happening, things that had happened before."

How right he was. Ballplayers like Willie Mays, Billy Williams, and an outfielder for the Giants named Bobby Bonds, who would later father one of the great home run hitters of all time, were in some cases the backbones of their teams. And yet, in urban America, things were very different from the playing fields. To many white Americans, these were still the cotton fields, and blacks were to be treated as such.

By the spring of 1970, there were student demonstrations, which had begun in earnest back in 1964, against the Viet Nam war, taking place on college campuses across the nation. During one such demonstration on the Jackson State College campus in Jackson, Mississippi, on May 14 and 15, police fired on a dormitory, killing two black students and wounding twelve more. This heartbreaking occurrence received minimal attention compared to the tragedy at Kent State University, ten days earlier. It became a point of reference for African American scholars who contended conditions had in fact not changed all that much.

But life for Christine and Byron would change in 1974, for the better. Lisa DeMorst, their first granddaughter was now seven and they were about to be blessed with another. Jackie had divorced her first husband and remarried. On May 22, she gave birth to Dominique Bozman. Byron and Christine now had two beautiful and sweet granddaughters to fawn over.

"There's nothing like grandkids," Byron said laughing. "You can spoil 'em rotten...then give them back to their mother."

And that's exactly what they did. It didn't take long for them to get lost in these two little girls. By the mid-1970s, Byron had retired from the bank job he'd taken after retiring from the post office and was now devoting full time to volunteer work at the church with various youth groups and, of course, was involved in their sports activities. Christine was still teaching, so they were both active and had found new happiness in Lisa and Dominique.

The 1970s would be a decade filled with diversity. America had landed on the moon, even ridden a buggy on the surface, but we also had a President resign before facing impeachment. The Viet Nam War officially ended as we withdrew our few remaining troops in April, 1975, two decades and nearly 60,000 dead, after we entered the country.

As was the history of the Civil Rights Movement, there was an ebb and flow during the 1970s. Killing and murder of blacks continued, but there was a conscious effort by people with a strong moral compass to make things right, give not only blacks, but all minorities their rightful chance. It was after all, the principles this country was founded on.

For Byron, Christine, Jackie, Lisa, and Dominique the remaining years of the 1970s would be tranquil. Their lives would be dominated by each other. Youth activities, school, church, and the celebration of life, their lives together, were what brought solitude and hope heading into the future.

17

As Byron and Christine entered their seventies, times were good for the Johnson family. Their lives had leveled, become quiet (except for the grand-daughters), and there was a sense of serenity.

"Our lives were peaceful," Byron recalled, "and we were enjoying life. We kept busy, I was working with the youth at the church, Christine was subbing (substitute teaching) and we spent lots of time with Lisa and Dominique...it was great."

As the Johnson family flourished, African Americans as a whole were not so lucky. In 1980, thirty-three percent of black males worked as professionals, managers and in sales, while 59% of white males worked in those same fields. Only 19% of black women worked professionally, with 32% of white women doing the same jobs. In 1985, 20.8 percent of black families earned less than

$15,000 compared to 10.4 percent of white families. But on the affirmative side of the ledger, the country had seen its first black governor (Douglas Wilder of Virginia), its first black woman astronaut (Dr. Mae Jemison, a medical doctor with a degree in chemical engineering), and Army General Colin R. Powell became the first African American to chair the Joint Chiefs of Staff; he also was the youngest man ever appointed to this position.

Baseball would have its ups and downs as well. The players' strike in 1981 forced the first split-season since 1892. Frank Robinson, who had become the first black manager in Major League history (Cleveland Indians – 1975), also became the first black manager in the National League, when he took the reins of the San Francisco Giants in 1981. Meanwhile, Pete Rose broke Ty Cobb's hitting record, by getting his 4,192nd base hit in Riverfront Stadium, in Cincinnati.

The decade would end with a World Series shortened by a massive earthquake in San Francisco Bay and that same Pete Rose being banned from baseball for allegedly gambling on the Reds, the team he managed.

Byron watched baseball from afar, but never lost interest in it. "I loved watching the games on TV. In some ways it had changed from the game I played, like the money these guys were making, but it was still a great game."

He may have been too old to play baseball, but having coached the women's softball team at the bank and now with Lisa turning out to be a pretty good basketball player, his interest in sports never waned.

Lisa attended Machebeuf High School and went out for varsity basketball her freshman year. She made the team, played one year, and quit to pursue her academics.

Lisa would forever be tied to Joe, probably because of her arrival and his leaving so closely connected. Jackie remembered one eerie birthday. "Right before her fourteenth birthday she came to me and said she was scared. I asked her why. She didn't know, she just thought she was going to die, but didn't know why she felt that way. She hadn't connected it to Joe, but you know, he died when he was fourteen...I don't know, it was just strange. I'll never forget it."

By 1990, Lisa was attending the University of Colorado at Boulder and Dominique was entering high school at Machebeuf. She, too, had developed into quite an athlete; however the sport she excelled at was volleyball. She would parlay her outstanding sports skill and grade point average into a four-year athletic scholarship to the University of the Pacific in Stockton, California. Again, she stood out and when the opportunity presented itself to try out for the 1996

Olympic Team in Atlanta, she took it.

"My father was like a dad to Lisa," Jackie commented. "He loved her playing basketball, but loved her doing well in school even more." And well she did, graduating and getting her degree from the University of Colorado – Denver.

"My grandfather was the major influence in me participating in volleyball," Dominique said fondly. "He started me playing when I was eleven years old, and never quit helping me my whole career."

Following the World University Games in Japan, she made the final cut for the U.S. Olympic volleyball team. Sadly, at the Olympic Festival showcase game in Colorado Springs, she broke her wrist. Her dream of an Olympic medal had ended.

As always her grandparents were there to let her know how proud they were of her. "No matter what happened, they were always there for Lisa and me. I'd always taken volleyball for granted, but after that incident...well, I guess I knew what I'd lost."

Dominique graduated from the University of the Pacific, went on and got her Master's degree from the University of Arkansas – Monticello and now teaches high school English at P.S. 1 in Denver. She has three beautiful children, Salih, a son born in 1998 and twins, Najah and Amir, 4, who along with Lisa's daughter, Desmarae, 12, are the apple of their great-grandfather's eye.

The Kansas City Monarchs seemed a million miles away for Byron now, and for all intents and purposes it was. Negro League baseball had, for the most part, died in 1947 when Jackie Robinson broke in with the Dodgers. It limped along for a few more years, actually surviving until 1960, but by 1955 it was legitimately finished. For the next 35 years, its memory remained in seclusion. Heartbreakingly, its history and its players had diminished to the point that not only did it appear no one cared, but nothing had really been done to recognize these men. They had become dinosaurs, ghosts of an era long since past, a time when THEIR game was thought to be desperate, and insignificant.

The irony of this was that some of the game's icons had gotten their starts during the twilight years of the Negro Leagues. Their forefathers had laid the groundwork for what was now the front line of the game that had turned its back on the pioneers of today's minority superstars.

By 1991, Major League baseball had apparently rediscovered these treasures of their past, and decided to acknowledge them. With enlightenment and exhausting research provided by such people as Robert

Peterson, *Only The Ball Was White*, Mark Ribowsky's, *A Complete History of the Negro Leagues*, as well as his books on Satchel Paige and Josh Gibson, probably the two greatest Negro League players who ever lived, and certainly, James Riley's *Biographical Encyclopedia of the Negro Baseball Leagues*, this lost history was suddenly not only being sought after, but being presented in an articulate and concise manner.

All were instrumental in this renaissance, along with an organization known as SABR (Society for American Baseball Research). Founded in 1971, it played a significant role in bringing the history of black baseball to light.

For Byron the word of this new discovery came from his daughter. Jackie had been visiting a family member, Rose Blaney, in Chicago in 1991 who'd mentioned to her she'd noticed in the *Chicago Defender*, a newspaper that had been around since the 1910s and had covered the old Negro Leagues, that Major League baseball was going to compensate black ballplayers who'd played in the Negro Leagues prior to 1947, when Jackie Robinson helped integrate the game. Byron definitely fit in this group.

"I called my father from Chicago and asked him if he'd heard anything about this," Jackie remarked. "He had no idea what I was talking about, and once I explained it, he said, 'I'll believe that when I see it,' and that was it for a while."

At age 81, on his birthday, and still playing golf, Byron got what every golfer in the world wants...a hole in one! Playing at City Park Golf Course in east Denver on a par three, bingo, his tee shot dropped in the cup. It's still not a subject you want to bring up around him, because, well, it's a long story, and he loves to tell it. The next day, however, he received a letter from Major League Baseball telling him they were in fact going to recompense him for those years he played Negro League baseball.

"He still didn't believe it was going to happen," Jackie said, "And even today when I take him the checks, he looks at them in disbelief."

In 1992, the Colorado Rockies were formed and local interest in baseball was at a fever pitch. Future Rockies fans couldn't get enough information, memorabilia, and/or anything that pertained to our national pastime.

On a sports talk show Tom Altherr, a college professor at Metropolitan State College of Denver, heard about Byron for the first time from a local sports reporter, Jim Armstrong. Since one of the courses Tom taught at Metro was Baseball History, he contacted Byron. They formed a lasting friendship, still active today. Byron, and usually Christine, would come and speak at Tom's classes.

"My students were captivated," Tom said. "Negro League baseball was...well, invisible. Byron brought it to life, they loved him."

Byron would start off, usually, by acknowledging Christine. "In high school, she always used to holler for me. Now she hollers at me." One of Christine's favorite stories was about the time Byron called her from the road and told her he was bringing the entire Monarch team home for dinner. For whatever reason Christine had never learned to cook that well.

"I was petrified. Here was the Kansas City Monarchs coming to our house and I didn't know what to do. I called my mother and she talked me through it over the phone, what to shop for, and how to cook it. I fixed a big beef roast and collard greens and some other side dishes. I was so nervous I had to take three showers. But everything worked out all right. Here came fifteen Monarchs, and we had a good time, all of them crowded in the dining room."

Around this same time a local, but well-known historian and authority on the Negro Leagues, Jay Sanford, befriended Byron. He arranged speaking engagements, even took Byron to Montana, where

Byron had once played, for a Negro League baseball celebration. This then led to newspaper articles, taped interviews, and recognition Byron never dreamed of.

As the Colorado Rockies entered their inaugural season, 1993, Byron was not only excited by the prospect of big league ball in Denver, but he felt to some extent he was part of it. Oh, not in the real active participation of it, but as a member of the baseball fraternity. He could look at these players and know he'd been one of those groundbreakers, a black ballplayer who'd paved a path for these modern day athletes who were reaping the rewards of those who had gone before. The fulfillment had come in small, measured doses, but nonetheless, had come.

Don Baylor was named the first manager of the Rockies, and there was a sense of pride in that for Byron. Baylor had missed the Negro Leagues by some fifteen years, but he was a man of history and appreciation. He knew what these men had done for his career, and felt an obligation to repay them in any way he could. He learned of Byron through media and organizational sources and contacted him.

"He called me and asked me if I'd be interested in throwing out the first ball at one of the games," Byron said smiling. "I couldn't believe it...I was honored."

In June, with a packed house at Mile High Stadium, Byron "Mex" Johnson walked to the mound, with various family members watching, and threw out the first pitch to start the game.

At age 82, the circumstances were a little different than in 1938 when he was an All-Star shortstop for the Kansas City Monarchs.

"Man, I'll tell you that home plate looked like it was a mile away. They let me stand in front of the mound on the grass...I got it in there, I guess I've still got that great arm," he said with a laugh.

In 1994, as Coors Field entered its final construction phases, Byron and Buck O'Neil, his friend and former teammate, were given a VIP tour of the ballpark by Baylor.

"Looking around at that park, well, it was somethin', nothin' like the ballparks we played in."

Byron would once again get to throw out the first ball, this time in 2000, at Coors Field, and again it was a special moment in the baseball life of one of the way makers.

All those miles, all those cities, the heartbreak of being treated and told you weren't as good, because you were black you were somehow inherently inferior.

Oh, but they knew different. They knew the baseball they were playing was not only equal, but very probably better. It was after all still a game, a boys' game played by men of passion and skill. Color didn't matter, throw, hit, run, it was all the same, whether in Wrigley Field or Muehlebach Stadium. Only white major league baseball found a reason to fear these men, and now, here on a warm summer afternoon, standing before baseball players and fans of every nationality, Byron's past seemed more distant than ever before. It was as if he'd come full circle.

As a young black ballplayer, he knew his place, where he was allowed to go and what he was allowed to do, but now, in this giant house, built to honor the game he so loved, HE was being honored.

18

Byron would have yet another mountain to climb in 1998. His beloved wife and lifetime partner, Christine would pass away.

"My father was on the golf course, when they came and got him," Jackie remembered. "My mother had gone upstairs for a musical recital in the their apartment building. When they called on her to sing, she couldn't get up out of the chair...they called an ambulance."

In September of 1997, one day after Byron's birthday, Christine would be taken to the hospital where tests were done. One of the tests showed she had a brain tumor, but it was on the outside of her brain so the doctors felt they could treat it with medication.

"I was in Madison (Wisconsin) when Carlotta called to tell me what happened," Jackie said. "I immediately flew home. When I walked into the hospital room, she looked fine. She didn't remember any of it. She told me she felt bad I'd come because she was okay."

In December, her symptoms had worsened, so more tests were done. They now found the tumor had grown and was moving inside her brain. Surgery was recommended.

"We were all home celebrating Christmas and then Kwanzaa, which starts the day after Christmas and runs to New Year," Jackie recalled. "We cut it short, because she was scheduled for surgery on the 28th. What none of us knew at the time was that Dominique was pregnant with Salih.

"You know my mom was a BIG Bronco fan, and when they were taking her in for surgery she said, 'Call Ron Zappolo (a local sportscaster at the time) and tell him to take care of the black boys!"

Christine came through the surgery fine, so Jackie went back to Madison, and Dominique went back to Arkansas. Lisa was there to help her grandfather and for a while things remained hopeful. Dominique's pregnancy was now known, and Christine would call her, have her hold the phone to her stomach so that she could sing to the baby.

"She had to go in for radiation treatments several

times a week," Jackie recalled, "And that's when she really started to slide."

By June, she was a shadow of what she once was. Byron had taken care of her to the point of exhaustion and his family began to worry about him. He was eighty-seven and the physical and emotional strain was taking a toll on him.

In July, the end came. She died peacefully. Her journey through life with Byron had been one of hardship and triumph. They weren't only husband and wife, but the best of friends, they'd shared everything together. They'd grown up together in Little Rock, survived World War II together, raised children together, and now he was alone. Oh, he had Jackie and his grandchildren, and even great grandchildren, but his soul-mate was gone. Only he knew what they had truly shared together. But as had always been the case with Byron, his faith and love of family kept him going.

Christine's funeral at Park Hill Methodist Church, in Denver, was a wonderful event. Family, friends, and many former students attended. Byron, Jackie, Lisa, and Dominique handled the sad occasion with great aplomb. It was a fitting testament to such a great woman.

Soon after Christine passed away, through the suggestion of Reverend Gilbert H. Caldwell at Park

Hill Methodist; the family started "The Christine Johnson Lecture Series," to explore the diversity and understanding of multicultural environments. That first year Byron was the keynote speaker. It was so well received that everyone involved wanted it to continue, but felt they should change the name. The second year it was renamed "The Byron and Christine Johnson Lecture Series," and has now been functioning for seven years. For the past four years this series has been offered as an accredited college course for students at Metropolitan State College of Denver.

Jackie and her daughter Dominique have in turn started Johnson Legacy Inc., a non-profit organization to further advance education in a multicultural setting, and in 2005 hope to kick off the "Mex" Johnson All-Stars, an after-school program at Stedman Elementary School.

In June of 2004, the Canadian Baseball Hall of Fame notified Byron he was being inducted. The ceremony took place in Saskatchewan in August. Unable to make it, Byron sent Carlotta in his place. He had recorded a five-minute acceptance speech, letting the people of Canada know how much he'd appreciated them as a black ballplayer. He is only one of two Negro League players in the Canadian hall of fame. The other is his good friend, Satchel Paige.

"It was a great honor," Byron stated happily. "They were always good to us in Canada. We liked playing there."

Today, Byron lives with his daughter Jackie, in the same apartment building he and Christine lived in. He has suffered some health setbacks, but his spirit is still intact.

His life has been exciting, discouraging, sad and exhilarating, but most of all it has been a journey through America. One man's and one family's voyage across the ball fields and cotton fields, the small family celebrations and national race riots, fighting for their right to be educated and fighting for their country. It is a passage like no other. They have survived, overcome, and triumphed. They should be respected and honored, not just as blacks, but as Americans. They've earned it!

"Most of us don't really believe our lives are so extraordinary as to warrant a book. Most of us focus on trying to get through life the best way we can. I am not extraordinary, but I guess I've had an extraordinary life. I say extraordinary because of the things I've experienced and the things I've been able to make it through. Some of them weren't pretty, and that stuff can get to you if you let it, but in spite of everything I had to go through – growing up down South, losing out on playing in the big leagues, fighting in a segregated army, and losing ones that were so dear to me – I still would have to say that I've had a good life. Not an easy life, but a good life. Now you might wonder why I say it's been a good life. Well, I still have pretty good health, and that's saying a lot at my age, and I still have my family... and I still have a pretty good golf swing."

Byron "Mex" Johnson - 2004

The Waymaker

These are his memories.
Here. Take this one about the soda pop tops used for baseballs in
    Little Rock
When the West End was more organic...unpaved roads and
    leaning, dripping trees.
Take the fading images of the way his mother's hair looked,
How she reined over gardens and dinner tables.
Take the memories of his father's hands presiding over paint brushes,
Jesus-like in his carpentry and his compassion.
Take the memories of a step-mother pushing him to go to college
In the comma of the Depression.
Not the ones of her after the stroke throwing her own sorrow at his face
Having no feeling left in her legs or in her heart.
Take the sparse memories of his sisters who had husbands
And children before he was even born
And the deep rolling memories of his brothers living epic lives the way
Black men in rural areas tend to.
Can you feel the memories of his son?
Gone at age fourteen from a disease they hadn't gotten around to
    thinking about yet.
Can you feel the landscape of memory he has of his wife?
Sixty years married, her brain tumor left him with not much to pour into
But the music of his daughter's smile and the contemplation of his
    own passing-
Which moves him out of bed still...
Positions him between this world and that one.
Can't keep a hold of his memories they are too numerous,
Too large, too entirely permissive.
He leaves them for those grandbabies to find in one of his sock drawers
Or under a baseball cap or tucked neatly in a large print Bible
The preacher gave him the Christmas before he broke his hip.
And that is all right.
That's a life do you hear me?
That is a life.

– Dominique C. Johnson

ACKNOWLEDGEMENTS

Where do you start acknowledging people and sources when writing a book that spans ninety plus years? I guess with the subject himself, Byron "Mex" Johnson.

I, unfortunately, didn't get to know Byron until the last few years. He was and is a remarkable man. I would first like to thank him for having such a remarkable life, and secondly, letting me be the one to tell his story. His daughter, Jackie Benton, was truly instrumental in getting this project going, supplying vital information, and having great patience as we made this journey.

Carlotta (Walls) LaNier played a significant role in not only helping to tell this story, but in obtaining President Bill Clinton to do the foreword. I would also like to thank Jackie's daughter, Dominique for her contributions.

Tom Altherr, not only provided information and insight, but did the editing as well. Several years ago, Jay Sanford, conducted some in depth interviews with Byron and fortunately recorded them. Those tapes played a key part in the writing of this book. I would also like to thank Buck O'Neil, who is without a doubt one of the most charismatic people I have ever met. Spending time with him talking about Byron and baseball in general are treasured moments. And, a very special thanks, to President Bill Clinton, and Don Baylor. Their contributions are immeasurable.

I would like to thank and acknowledge the following research sources for their input in this book. The *Kansas City Monarchs* by Janet Bruce, *Blackball Stars* by John Holway, *The Negro Leagues Revisited* by Brent Kelley, *The Negro Leagues Book* by Dick Clark & Larry Lester, *Jackie's Nine* by Sharon Robinson, *Maybe I'll Pitch Forever* by Satchel Paige, *Don't Look Back* by Mark Ribowsky, *The Power and the Darkness* by Mark Ribowsky, *Only the Ball Was White* by Robert Peterson, *A Complete History of the Negro Leagues* by Mark Ribowsky, *I Was Right On Time* by Buck O'Neil, *The Biographical Encyclopedia of the Negro Baseball Leagues* by James Riley, *20th Century Baseball Chronicle* by David Nemec, Stephen Hanks, Dick Johnson, David Raskin, Thomas Gilbert, Andy Cohen, Joe Glickman, Danny Green and Stuart Shea. *Rediscovering America* by Carla Blank and the *Denver Post* Newspaper. Also, a special thanks to *BASEBALL*, A Film by Ken Burns.

To my mom, Dixie Sumner, who passed away during the writing of this book – I Love You!

Jan Sumner - 2005

ABOUT THE AUTHOR

Jan Sumner was born in Independence, Kansas, but has spent his entire life in Denver, Colorado. He is a graduate of Metropolitan State College in Denver. He has been active in baseball his entire life and in 1993 started throwing batting practice for the Colorado Rockies. He threw for them through the 1999 season and wrote a book about his experiences called *Fat Pitch*, published in 2001. It's an insightful and humorous behind the scenes look at the Rockies from their first days at Mile High Stadium through their first four years at Coors Field. He then wrote a murder mystery, *Death Camass*, about a serial killers reach from the grave, haunting lives twenty years after his death. He started his own publishing company, JaDan Publishing, at that time, and is now publishing books for other authors.

Jan's latest work is *Legacy of a Monarch*, the biography of Byron "Mex" Johnson, an All-Star Negro League baseball player of the 1930s–1940s. It is a history of not only a black baseball player, but of an African American's journey through American history.

Jan has also co-authored and published, *Face to Face With Sports Legends* by Joe Cullinane, *When Pro Football Was Fun* by Vic Boccard, and *The Mental Side of Hitting* by Mike Epstein.